3-54

OUTCOME OF BLACK CHILDREN — WHITE PARENTS TRANSRACIAL ADOPTIONS

CHARLES H. ZASTROW

San Francisco, California
1977

Published By

R&E RESEARCH ASSOCIATES, INC.
4843 Mission Street
San Francisco, California 94112

Publishers

Robert D. Reed and Adam S. Eterovich

HV
875
.Z37

Library of Congress Card Catalog Number
76-56070

I.S.B.N.
0-88247-456-1

ACKNOWLEDGMENTS

I owe my first debt to Dr. Alfred Kadushin, my major professor, for his guidance, suggestions, and conscientious supervision through the course of my studies. My sincere appreciation is also extended to Professors Melvin Brenner, John Flanagan, Ersel Le Masters, and Harry Sharp.

Without the help, inspiration, and plain hard work of many other people, this study would have have been completed. The author wishes to express his gratitude to the adoption agencies and to the Wisconsin Division of Family Services (State Department of Health and Social Services) for their cooperation in selecting the study group and collecting the study data. Among the agency people who did much of the work were Jules Bader, Miss Geraldine Beyerstett, Miss Cecilia Braam, Miss Julia Boyce, Lowell Grottveit, Robert Hintz, Miss Kay Leonhardt, Mrs. Edna Levis, and Norman Schuett. A special note of thanks goes to Miss Verna Lauritzen who coordinated the activities of agencies in selecting the study group, and who also contributed valuable suggestions for the design of the study. Without her help, the project could not have been conducted.

The personnel of the Wisconsin Survey Research Laboratory were very helpful in designing the interview schedules. The interviewers for the project are to be thanked for doing a commendable job. Special appreciation is extended to the study group families for their willingness to participate.

A different kind of debt is owed to Mrs. Judy Saviano and Mrs. Evie Coffman who cheerfully and voluntarily helped prepare much of the material for the study.

Finally, as is frequently the case, but not less worthy because of it, the last acknowledgment must go to my wife, Kay, who types the manuscript, and provided her warm companionship through the writing of the study.

iii

TABLE OF CONTENTS

LIST OF TABLES

I now know there are no unadoptable children.

None? Well, perhaps one exception must be made. The child whose
mixture is Negro and white is still too often homeless when he is
orphaned by death or desertion. Are such children to be without
home and parents? There are not enough Negro families able to
adopt them. Yet there are many white families who long for children and for whom there are none .... Time and again we have
proved that race and religion do not matter. All that matters is
the ability to love. I know, for I have tried it myself. My own
youngest child is half-Negro, born of an American Negro father in
Germany and a German mother. Yes, the first few days I did notice
when I bathed her that her skin was darker than my own. The first
day perhaps I felt it was strange. But caring for that little body,
watching the keen quick mind awaken and develop, enjoying the
gaiety and the vigor of the personality, soon made the child my own.
Her flesh became my flesh by love, and we are mother and child.
Does she fit into our home? Yes, because she is so much like me.
I see myself when I was a child in so many of her ways. I could not
have created a child more like me than she is, because we have the
same kind of mind and heart. Parenthood has nothing to do with
color, race or religion. (pp. 91-92)

(Pearl S. Buck, 1964)

CHAPTER I

INTRODUCTION

Role of Adoption

Adoption provides substitute care (parents) for children whose natural parents
are unable or unwilling to care for them. As a legal proceeding of the court, it in-
volves permanent transfer of parental rights from the natural parents to the adopters.
A more formal definition of adoption indicates, "It entails the extinction of all
present or future rights and obligations of the natural parents and the transfer, by
administrative or legal authority, of all these rights and obligations to a married
couple who have no blood relationship with the child." (Toussieng, 1962; p. 63).

In our society it is generally assumed adoptive placement is the most satisfactory solution for providing care to children whose natural parents are unable to
fulfill this role (Pringle, 1967). Other alternative forms of substitute care include institutional and foster care. Adoption is not a recent development as adoptions are recorded among such ancient civilizations as the Babylonians, Egyptians,
Greeks and Romans. The Bible, for example, mentions Pharoah's daughter adopted Moses
and Mordecai adopted Esther.

Adoptions in the United States are regulated by state statutes. The first state
to introduce adoption legislation was Massachusetts in 1851. At present, every state
has an adoption statute, and Friedlander (1968) notes the objectives of such legislation are:

One objective of adoption law is to protect the child from unnecessary
separation from his natural parents; from adoption by unfit parents;

1

and from interference by his natural parents after a successful adoption has been arranged. Another objection is to protect the natural parents, particularly the unmarried mother, from unwise decisions made under emotional stress or economic pressure, which they might greatly regret later. Still another is to protect the adopting parents from taking a permanent responsibility for children whose health, heredity, or physical and mental capacities might lead to their disappointment, and also to protect them from disturbance of their relationship with the adopted child by threats or blackmail from the natural parents. (p. 380)

Adoptions can be categorized into two types, relative (children adopted by relatives or by a step-parent) and nonrelative (children unrelated to the adopting couples). In 1968 there were 166,000 adoptions in the United States approved by the courts, 86,300 or 52% were nonrelative adoptions. Of the nonrelative adoptions, 74% were agency adoptions and 26% were independent adoptions (Child Welfare Statistics-- 1968).

Adoption serves two main functions: one is parent-centered, to provide children to married couples wanting children or additional children; and the other is child-centered, to provide families for parentless children. The latter function is now considered the most important (Child Welfare League of America, 1968), with the result being that in arranging adoptive placements, the primary concern of courts and adoption agencies is to meet the needs of the children.

Because of the values in our society, prospective adoptive couples have primarily been interested in adopting white infants who are physically and mentally healthy. For such parentless infants there has been and continues to be more adoptive applicants than there are children available. However, for children who are different (older, physically or mentally impaired, or nonwhite) there are many more children available for adoption than there are applicants. Such children are considered hard-to-place, with the largest group being nonwhite, primarily Black (Kadushin, 1967).

Statement of Problem

Finding homes for the large number of Black and mixed-Black children who are available for adoption is one of the more serious problems in the child welfare field. Although accurate data has not been compiled on the number of Black children available for adoption, Marmor (1964) notes in New York City well over 50% of all children who need placement are Black, and the Children, a Bureau (Riday, 1969) estimates there are between 40,000 and 80,000 Black children available for adoption for whom an adoptive home cannot be found.

A recent survey (Grow, 1970) of 261 public and voluntary agencies in the United States found an appreciable surplus of approved white homes in relation to the number of white children available for adoption (116 per 100); and a severe shortage of approved nonwhite homes in relation to the number of nonwhite available children (39 per 100). In addition, there is evidence that the number of Black children known to agencies as available for adoption may only be a small fraction of the number that would be available if there were more adoptive applicants. The Detroit News (Feb. 23, 1964), for example, reported in 1964 that the 99 Black children available for adoption in that city were only a small proportion of those really needing adoptive homes. The court had over 1500 children in custody for whom it was thought the natural parental rights could be terminated, thereby making these children legally free for adoption. But no effort was being made to do so as there was little prospect of finding adoptive parents.

2

Because of the difficulty of finding adoptive parents, adoption agencies have in the past been reluctant to accept responsibility for care and placement of Black children, and frequently have encouraged Black unwed mothers to keep their babies (Child Welfare League of America, 1968). Statistically, Black unwed mothers are much more likely to keep their babies than unwed white mothers. A study in New York City, for instance, found 19.7% of the white children born out-of-wedlock are kept by their mothers, while 78.4% of Black children are kept by their unwed mothers (Citizens' Committee for Children of New York, 1963). One of the major reasons Black unmarried mothers are much more apt to keep their babies appears to be due to an awareness there are few adoptive homes for their babies (Kadushin, 1967). Adams & Gallagher (1963) found 70% of the white babies born out-of-wedlock in the United States are adopted, while only 5% of out-of-wedlock Black babies are adopted. It may well be if there were a significant increase in adoptive applicants for Black children, unwed Black mothers would be more willing to place their children for adoption.

The gap between the number of available Black children and the number of Black adoptive applicants appears to be more of a problem of disproportionate supply than of lagging demand. Black couples are adopting at a rate about equal to the rate for white couples. Child Welfare Statistics--1968 show 78,500 white couples and 7,800 nonwhite couples adopted children unrelated to them in 1968. Since the nonwhite population is approximately one-tenth of our total population (U.S. Census Bureau estimated the nonwhite population in 1969 was 12.3%), nonwhites are adopting at a rate close to the rate of whites. In studies conducted by the Children's Bureau (Herzog & Bernstein, 1965), where adjustment was made for family composition (husband-wife families, with heads under 45 years of age), it was found that

> ... the ratio of non-relative adoptions was 3 per 1000 couples for all races combined and also for the white population. For Negro husband-wife families of the same age, it was 2.7, only a little lower. When income (over $3000) was considered as well, ... the adoption ratio for the United States in 1961, for all races combined, rose from 3 children adopted by non-relatives per 1000 husband-wife families with heads under 45 to 3.5 per 1000 such families. For white families, the ratio rose only from 3 to 3.4. But for nonwhite families, it rose to 4.9. Apparently, either those nonwhite families having higher incomes were more likely than white families to adopt children not related to them, or a significant number of nonwhite families with incomes under $3000 adopted children--or possibly both. Thus it appears that the lower proportion of two-parent families found among Negroes, and the notoriously low-income levels so prevalent in this minority group, fully account for the dearth of Negro adoptive applicants, without any need to assume different attitudes towards adoption. (It should be remembered also that we are discussing here only legal adoptions, leaving aside informal arrangements of child care which are not legalized.) (p. 17)

The disproportionate supply of parentless Black children is indicated in the following statistics. Child Welfare Statistics--1968 show 88% of children adopted by unrelated petitioners were born out-of-wedlock. Although nonwhites constitute only about one-tenth of the population in the United States, there are annually more illegitimate nonwhite births than white. Table 1 helps to make this clear, and also shows a significant increase in births out-of-wedlock since World War II.

Although these statistics on out-of-wedlock births are sometimes seized upon to support the image of widespread pathology, rampant sexuality, and galloping family disintegration among Blacks, it should be noted such deductions may be hasty as other factors also affect the illegitimacy rate. White women are more likely to use birth

3

Table 1

ILLEGITIMATE LIVE BIRTHS IN U.S. BY RACE OF MOTHER
1940-1968

Year	Total Out-of-Wedlock Births	White	Black and Other	Percent Black and Other
1940	89,500	40,300	49,200	55.0
1945	117,400	56,400	60,900	51.9
1950	141,600	53,500	88,100	62.2
1955	183,000	64,200	119,200	65.0
1960	224,300	82,500	141,800	63.2
1965	291,200	123,700	167,500	57.5
1966	302,400	132,700	169,500	56.1
1967	318,100	142,200	175,800	55.3
1968	339,200	155,200	183,900	54.2

Source: Bureau of the Census, U.S. Department of Commerce,
Statistical Abstract of the United States, 1970,
Washington, D.C.: Government Printing Office, p. 50.

control devices (Rainwater and Weinstein, 1960), more apt to find ways to avoid regis-
tering out-of-wedlock births (Roberts, 1966), more likely to terminate an out-of-wedlock
pregnancy with an abortion (Schur, 1965), and more likely to marry before the birth of
the child (Herzog, 1964).

These reasons do not dismiss the fact, however, that a large number of Black children are born in a status branded as illegitimate, and that many of these children are
not being raised in a permanent family setting. The second choice for raising these
children has been in a foster home (sometimes a succession of foster homes) or in an
institution.

In recent years a number of adoption agencies in the United States and Canada have
attempted to more fully meet this need by placing Black and part-Black children with
white couples. The Children's Service Centre of Montreal pioneered, beginning in 1958,
in this type of transracial placement (Mitchell, 1969). In the first 10 years of the
program, over 200 Black children were placed in white homes by this agency (Open Door
Society, 1968). In addition, a number of organizations have been formed to share and
exchange information among transracial adoptive families, and to recruit additional
adoptive couples for Black children. Such organizations include OPPORTUNITY in Portland, Oregon; PAMY (Parents to Adopt Minority Youngsters) in Minnesota; Inter-Racial
Families in Madison, Wisconsin; and Open Door Societies in the United States and Canada.
Adoption resource exchanges are also being set up throughout the country to assist in
linking hard-to-place children with adoptive applicants.

In order to obtain an estimate of the number of Black children placed for adoption, and to obtain information on the number of these placements which are interracial, OPPORTUNITY (1970) undertook a survey of approximately 500 agencies, including
all state welfare departments and many county welfare departments in states having
no central reporting systems. The number of Black children placed in 1969 were surveyed. Responses were received from 342 agencies, with 210 agencies indicating they
had placed Black children in white facilities. OPPORTUNITY estimated that the total

4

number of Black placements in this survey represents as much as 90% of all agency placements of Black children in 1969. The results of the survey are presented by state in Table 2.

Table 2

CHILDREN OF BLACK ANCESTRY PLACED FOR ADOPTION IN 1969
(Report of Survey Conducted by OPPORTUNITY)

State	Number of Agencies	Children Placed	
		Black Homes	White Homes
Alabama[1]	1	5	0
Alaska	1	7	3
Arizona	4	23	5
Arkansas[1]			
California[2]	6	413	308
Colorado	4	29	20
Connecticut	9	51	28
Delaware[3]	2	22	5
Dist. of Columbia	4	111	11
Florida	5	85	0
Georgia	2	102	2
Hawaii[4]			
Idaho[4]			
Illinois[5]	25	234	75
Indiana[1]	10	26	18
Iowa[1]	14	36	39
Kansas	2	24	4
Kentucky	3	29	5
Louisiana	2	44	0
Maine[1]	3	0	2
Maryland	12	72	17
Massachusetts	16	32	97
Michigan	16	251	61
Minnesota	9	29	170
Mississippi	1	23	0
Missouri	5	27	10
Montana	2	2	1
Nebraska	4	11	9
Nevada	1	6	2
New Hampshire	3	2	17
New Jersey	8	98	29
New Mexico	2	11	10
New York	31	321	100
North Carolina[1]	1	20	0
North Dakota[3]	3	4	7
Ohio	33	213	36
Oklahoma	4	34	3
Oregon	7	39	65
Pennsylvania[6]	36	141	51
Rhode Island	4	13	11
South Carolina[1]	1	1	0
South Dakota	2	2	0

5

Table 2 (Concluded)

State	Number of Agencies	Children Placed	
		Black Homes	White Homes
Tennessee	4	51	2
Texas	9	93	5
Utah	4	5	4
Vermont	4	2	8
Virginia[3]	5	25	2
Washington	7	58	106
West Virginia	1	20	6
Wisconsin	8	35	87
Wyoming	2	7	6
Total	342	2,889	1,447

NOTES:

1. No report received from State Department of Public Welfare or other public agencies.

2. The 308 children reported as placed in white homes includes 33 children who were placed with families who were "mixed racial," but were not black or part black.

3. Public welfare does not have an adoption program.

4. State Department does not list children placed for adoption by race, but indicates black or part black children are very few.

5. No report from state welfare department. Figures include reports from several counties, although Cook County not included.

6. State welfare department does not place children for adoption. Figures include reports from several county agencies.

Source: Table appeared in Opportunity, Vol. 6, July-August 1970, Portland, Oregon. Reproduction of table was authorized by OPPORTUNITY.

Table 2 shows the survey by OPPORTUNITY found 4,336 Black children placed in 1969, with 1,447 (33%) being in white families. OPPORTUNITY conducted a similar survey on Black placements in 1968, and found that 23% of the Black placements were in white homes. These results show a significant increase in interracial placements for 1969, and also suggest if interracial placements continue to substantially increase in the future, there will be hope of achieving permanent family care for the large number of Black children available for adoption. (The need for adoptive families for Black children is also indirectly indicated by the 1968 OPPORTUNITY survey which found that children of Black ancestry represent only about half of all the nonwhite children placed for adoption, even though Blacks represent 90% of the nonwhite population.)

Despite these concerted efforts, the number of Black children available for adoption continues to far exceed the number of adoptive applicants. There are still a number of unanswered questions about the outcome of such transracial placements that may be deterring potential white adoptive applicants from applying; and which prompt some adoption agencies, social workers, judges, attorneys, and referral sources to be cautious about encouraging such transracial placements. Among the questions for which there is at best only limited information are the following. Can Black children be accepted by white couples as sons and daughters? What problems are encountered by the parents, the adopted child, and other siblings in the family? What are the reactions of relatives, friends, neighbors, strangers and the broader community to the adoption? What satisfactions are derived by the adoptive family? How do the experiences of interracial adoptive families compare to experiences of intraracial adoptive families? In what ways are interracial adoptive couples different from intraracial adoptive couples? Why do white couples want to adopt a Black child? Will the adopted Black child, reared in a white family, and perhaps also in a white community, experience difficulty in establishing a self-identity? As the Black child grows older, what problems, if any, will be encountered in school, in dating, and in seeking employment? Information on these specific questions will be pertinent in providing an answer to the more global question about such placements, "Is the overall outcome of Black-white transracial placements successful, and to be encouraged by the field of social welfare?"

Study Objectives and Significance

The two objectives of this study are to,

(1) Identify the specific satisfactions derived and difficulties encountered by white parents who adopted a Black child.

(2) Assess the overall outcome of white couples--Black children adoptions.

The specific procedures for conducting the study will be discussed in the next chapter, but the general design of the study is to compare (through interviews with adoptive parents and reading of adoption record material) the experiences of a group of white couples who adopted a Black child to the experiences of a comparison group of white couples who adopted a child of their own race. Because such transracial placements have only occurred in recent years, the children in the study group are of preschool age. Therefore, the study will only provide information on the outcome during the first few years following placement.

The significance of this study is primarily related to the large number of parentless Black children. If research on transracial placements finds that the overall outcome is not desirable, such placements should probably be discontinued or used only in rare cases, with the implication being that parentless Black children for whom Black adoptive applicants cannot be found, will need to be placed in foster homes and institutions; a second choice that is generally considered less desirable than adoption for the child's growth and development (Pringle, 1967), and which is also a considerable expense to taxpayers.

If on the other hand the overall outcome is shown to be desirable, such transracial placements are to be encouraged and it offers some hope of more fully meeting the need of finding parents for the large number of Black children available for adoption. Although this particular study will certainly not be the definitive study and answer all the questions that have been raised, it will provide some indication of the outcome during the first few years following placement. In addition, if evidence of a successful overall outcome is found, information on the specific satisfactions derived and problems encountered by transracial adoptive parents should be useful in recruiting prospective transracial applicants and in providing information about what the future is likely to hold if a Black child is adopted. For adoption workers, the study may pinpoint certain problem situations and considerations in reference to transracial adoptions that should be explored with prospective transracial adoption applicants.

The study also has significance as it relates to the racial issue which has been a central point of national concern for a number of years. Black children-white parents transracial adoptions bring into contrast the two polar races in our society, black and white. The past 15 years has seen an upsurge of self-consciousness and movement toward equal rights for the American Black, and discrimination barriers are being attacked on many fronts. A concerted effort has been made by recent presidential administrations, by Congress, by the judicial system, and by civil rights organizations to upgrade the status of Blacks and provide equal opportunities. Despite these efforts, with the increasing polarization of our society, it is difficult to assess whether we are moving closer to integration or to separation. It is possible that research on transracial placements may reveal aspects of such placements that could be fuel for the fires of either separationists or integrationists.

Fanshel (1966) who is presently completing a longitudinal outcome study on American Indian children placed for adoption with white parents, made the following observations about the significance of Black-white transracial adoptions,

For the student of the American social scene, the degree to which such adoptions can be undertaken by couples and successfully sustained tells us something about where we are headed as a nation with respect to our feelings about race and ethnicity. That this is still a matter for conjecture was recently highlighted in the national press when a white minister and his wife returned a Negro baby to an adoption agency, reporting persistent adverse pressure by the community as a basis for their decision. (pp. 2-3)

CHAPTER II

STUDY DESIGN

Synopsis of Design

Two groups of families compose the study group; a group of 44 white couples who
adopted a child of their own race. The study data on the outcome of the adoptive
experiences were obtained by an interview held in the home of the adoptive parents,
and by reading the agency adoptive record material on these families. In order to
attempt to decrease the effect of confounding variables, the two groups were matched
on the age of the adopted child, and on the socio-economic status of the adoptive
parents. Two additional requirements for inclusion in the study group were that the
adoption needed to be finalized, and the child had to be no older than six years of
age.

Racial Classification

In regards to the racial categorization of a child, it should be noted there are
no clearly delineating biological classifications of races (see e.g., Richmond, 1954;
Haring, 1962; and Montagu, 1964). Despite definitional problems, it is necessary in
social research to use racial categories as race has important (though not necessarily
consistent) social meanings for people. In order to have a basis for racial classifications, a number of social scientists have used a social rather than a biological
definition; i.e., the way in which members of society classify each other by physical
characteristics (Marden and Meyer, 1962). A frequently used social definition of a
Black in America is anyone displaying any Negroid characteristics or anyone having any
known Black ancestry (see e.g., Rose, 1964; Pettigrew, 1964; and Berry, 1965). The
sociological classification of races is indicated by different definitions of a race
among various societies; for example, in the United States anyone who is not pure white
and is known to have Black ancestry is called a Black; while in Brazil anyone who is
not pure black is classified as white (Ehrlich & Holm, 1964).

It should also be noted that varying degrees of Negroid characteristics in part-
Black children (such as skin coloring, and texture of hair) may evoke somewhat different social meanings to persons (Warner & Srole, 1945). The ancestry of a child
sometimes also has different social meanings; e.g., directors of adoption agencies
informed the writer that a baby born of one parent who is black and the other white
is much less acceptable to the Black community than a baby of the "same racial composition" whose parents are both mulatto.

For the purpose of this study, a Black child will be one who is classified by adoption agencies as being "Black" or "mixed-Black." Directors of agencies in the State
(Wisconsin) in which the study was conducted indicated the "mixed-Black" label is
likely to be assigned to children whose racial composition is a mixture of 1/8 or more
"Black" and some other race. In this report the term "Black" will generally be used
for the sake of brevity to refer to both the Black and mixed-Black children in the
study group.

Choice of Comparison Group

During the design development phase of this study, several different groups were
considered before choosing as the comparison group white couples who adopted a white

9

child. Alternatives considered included Black children in foster care or institutions, Black children being raised by their natural parents, white children being raised by their natural parents, white children adopted by Black couples, and Black children adopted by Black couples.

Black children in foster care or institutions was not chosen as the comparison group as such care is generally considered somewhat less desirable for a child's growth and development than adoptive care (Pringle, 1967). It should be noted, however, that if research indicates the outcome of interracial adoptive placements is somewhat less desirable than intraracial placements, it would be very worthwhile to compare the outcome of interracial adoptive placements to that of placing Black children in foster care or institutions, since this is the primary alternative to adoption for the large number of parentless Black children.

Neither Black children being raised by their natural parents nor white children being raised by their natural parents were chosen as comparison groups as there is some research evidence of poorer adjustment among adopted children. Nemovicher (1959) investigated differences in personality characteristics between adopted boys and boys in the homes of their biological parents; the adopted boys were found to be significantly more hostile, tense, dependent and fearful. Brown (1958) found that adopted children showed, on several projective tests, more anxiety about parental attitudes and about punishment than control subjects. Witmer and associates (1963) found adopted children showed a slightly poorer adjustment than a control group of children living with their natural parents; however, when those adopted after the first month of life were excluded, there was almost no difference between the two groups in adjustment.

White children adopted by Black couples was excluded from consideration as a comparison group when it was discovered there have been no placements of this type in Wisconsin, and perhaps more (or at least very few) in the United States. Although such a comparison group may be interesting in that Black children-white parents transracial adoptions would be compared to the reverse type, white children-Black parents; such a comparison would only lead to a determination of white type of transracial placement is more successful. It would not provide an answer to how successful transracial placements are in comparison to intraracial placements or to alternative forms of substitute care. Comparing Black children-white parents transracial adoptions to intraracial placements would appear to be a more important comparison at this time in order to determine if this type of transracial placement is an acceptable form of care for the large number of parentless Black children.

Black children adopted by Black couples was given careful consideration as a choice for the comparison group. Similar to the comparison group chosen (white children adopted by white parents) it would have had the desired effect of comparing transracial placements to intraracial placements. One of the reasons for the selection of the white children-white parents group is that there has been considerable research on this group demonstrating the outcome of such placements is quite successful (see e.g., Kadushin's Review, 1967; a summary of the research results will also be presented in a later chapter). It was felt that using this control group provided a high, proven standard of outcome that would be a good test for comparing the outcome of these transracial placements. Although the outcome of Black children adopted by Black couples may well be as successful as white children-white parents adoptions, the writer is unaware of any research that has been conducted on the outcome of such placements. For the purposes of this study it was considered important to have baseline data indicating the successfulness of the outcome of the control group placements. If resources would have been available, the Black children-Black parents group would have been included as an additional comparison group. An additional reason for the choice made for the comparison group is that the primary focus of the study (as will be expanded upon in the next section) is on the parents' satisfactions with their adoptive experiences. With this focus on parental satisfaction, the choice of the parents in the comparison group being white is perhaps more appropriate; if there are differences in parental satisfactions associated with the race of the parent, selecting white parents for the control group would eliminate differences due to race from influencing the results.

One further clarification in regards to the selection of the comparison group perhaps should be made. The question may be raised, "Why include white children-white parents adoptions as a comparison group when the success rate of these adoptions has been documented in prior studies?" The reason is that outcome results are somewhat dependent on the outcome criterion employed and on the instruments used to measure outcome. Therefore, in order to control for such variations, it was considered important to have a comparison group in which the outcome of these adoptions would be assessed by the same study procedures and instruments as used for the transracial group.

Choice of Outcome Criterion

As indicated earlier, the outcome criterion used in this study is parental satisfaction with adoptive experience. In contrast to personality functioning assessment (which is the criterion used most frequently in outcome studies in the social sciences), parental satisfaction focuses attention on social functioning and social role performance. Kadushin (1966) notes in determining the success of a placement an adoptive child's "personality adjustment" may be secondary in importance to the parental satisfaction with the child. It is possible for an adoptive placement to be successful (i.e., provide satisfaction to both the child and his adoptive parents) even though the child may not be "well-adjusted" or "psychologically healthy."

Unlike the personality adjustment criterion, the satisfaction criterion gives attention to fulfillment of individual needs of the child and his adoptive parents. The importance of need fulfillment is underlined by Colvin (1962) who found that the best foster child-parent relationships were not necessarily those in which the parents fit the ideal picture of the good parent. "Instead it was strikingly evident that successful placements do occur with the correct matching of specific assets and defects on the part of both parents and children" (p. 46).

The acceptability of the parental satisfaction criterion is also indicated by the close relationship it has been found to have with personality adjustment in prior adoptive outcome studies (see e.g., Witmer, 1963; Wittenborn, 1957; Fanshel & Jaffe, 1965). One reason for the close association may be that psychologically "healthy" people are apt to perform their roles adequately. Since agencies and the broader community are more likely to see adoption as primarily a service to the child rather than to the parents, they may be more interested in outcome in terms of child adjustment. Because of the close association between parental satisfaction and personality adjustment, adoption agencies have some assurance that if a high level of parental satisfaction is demonstrated in research of this type, a satisfactory adjustment of the children can also be expected.

The focus on parental reaction to the adoptive experience can also be justified because of the recruitment need to find parents for the large number of Black children available for adoption. Prospective white adoptive parents for Black children are apt

11

to be primarily concerned with satisfactions they are likely to derive and difficulties they are apt to encounter if they decide to adopt a Black child. Such applicants are apt to want to know, and need to be told what have been the experiences of other white parents who adopted a Black child. Therefore, adoption agencies should have this information available for their work with applicants. In addition, if the outcome of such transracial placements is found to be a highly satisfying personal experience for parents, such a finding should be valuable in recruitment efforts to interest parents who have never thought about adopting.

Procedures for Selection of Study Group

As mentioned earlier, two groups compose the study group; a group of white parents who adopted a Black child, and a matched comparison group of white parents who adopted a child of their own race. The two groups were matched on age of adopted child, and on the socio-economic status of the adoptive parents. Two additional requirements for inclusion in the study group were that the child had to be no older than six years and that the adoption needed to be finalized. The Wisconsin Adoption Statute requires court permission be obtained before adoption agencies can provide names and other identifying information on adoptive families to anyone other than staff of child welfare agencies. When designing the study it was assumed judges would not grant the necessary legal permission unless the adoptive families indicated a willingness to participate in the study. But the researcher, of course, was not permitted to receive the names of the adoptive families and therefore could not directly contact the families to find out if they were willing to participate. In order to determine if adoptive parents were willing to participate, arrangements were made to have the adoption agencies that placed the children contact the adoptive couples. The following highly involved and complicated procedures were developed and employed in selecting the study group.

Step 1): The proposal for the study was submitted to the Wisconsin Division of Family Services (a Division of the State Department of Health and Social Services), and their approval for the study to be conducted was obtained. The Division of Family Services then identified the adoption agencies in the State which in recent years had placed Black children with white families for adoption.

Step 2): A meeting was held with these adoption agencies in which the nature and procedures of the study were outlined. The general consensus was that the objectives of the study had merit, and the agencies indicated their willingness to assist in the selection of the study group.

Step 3): Each adoption agency identified the Black children (whose birth dates were between January 1, 1964 and March 31, 1969) it had placed for adoption with white couples, and for whom the adoption had been finalized. The State Division of Family Services assisted in this identification process by sending a list to each agency of the Black children that the State's records showed had been placed by that agency during the indicated time period. The list contained the Black children placed with white parents as well as those placed with Black parents, as the State does not routinely compile information on the race of the parents who adopted Black children. The following nine agencies identified Black children placed with white families who met the above mentioned criteria:

Catholic Social Service in Madison
Catholic Social Service in Milwaukee
Children's Service Society of Wisconsin

Lutheran Social Services of Wisconsin and Upper Michigan
Milwaukee County Public Welfare Department
The Green Bay, Madison, Milwaukee, and Rhinelander Regional Offices for the
  State Division of Family Services

Step 4): To every white adoptive couple of a Black child identified as meeting
the criteria for the study group, the respective adoption agency sent a letter explaining the nature and sponsorship of the project, and asking if they would be
willing to share their adoptive experiences with an interviewer. (A sample letter
used by agencies as a guide in composing the letter to the transracial adoptive parents is contained in the Appendix.) In order to facilitate the parents' reply, the
agencies sent, along with each letter, a reply card with a self-addressed return
envelope to the agency.

Step 5): For each Black child whose adoptive parents indicated a willingness to
participate in the study, the respective adoption agency identified from its files
ten white children placed by the agency whose adoptions had been finalized and whose
birthdates were within four months of the birthdate of the Black child. For each
Black and respective white children identified, the agencies specified on the following form the case numbers and birthdates of the children, and the occupations and
last grade in school completed by the adoptive fathers. Upon completing these forms
the agencies sent the forms to the researcher.

Step 6): The information on these forms was used to match pair-by-pair an intraracial adoptive family to a transracial adoptive family. The matching procedures were
as follows: The Occupation Scale developed by Warner et al. (Miller, 1964) was used
to categorize the occupations into seven different socio-economic levels. (A copy of
the Occupation scale is presented in Appendix D.) This scale has been used exten-
sively to measure socio-economic status in social research. In an attempt to assess
the validity of the Occupation Scale, Kahl & Davis (1955) compared the scale to 18
other single measures of socio-economic status; and found a product moment correlation of .74 between occupation and status of friends, and a multiple correlation of
.80 between occupation plus education and status of friends. Kahl & Davis conclude,
"... our data agree with Warner's that occupation (as he measures it) is the best in-
dicator of either social participation or the whole socio-economic cluster represented
by the general factor identified by factor analysis" (p. 324). After reviewing research
studies on various indices of socio-economic status, Miller (1964) concludes;

> The Occupation Scale is the best single predictor of social class position
> within a seven point range. The high correlation it exhibits with the
> evaluative participative method of social class position (r = .91) commends
> occupation as a single dimension. Researchers will achieve a high degree
> of predictive efficiency by use of the one scale. (p. 102)

Following the ranking of the adoptive fathers' occupations into the seven socio-
economic levels, the scale level assigned to the adoptive father of each Black child
was noted. The intraracial adoptive fathers whose rankings did not differ by more
than one scale point from the interracial adoptive fathers were considered as possible
matches. Of these intraracial adoptive fathers, the one whose number of school years
completed was most similar to the transracial adoptive father was selected to be the
match. (Data on the education and occupation of the families in the study group are
presented in the next chapter.)

Step 7): Upon matching an intraracial adoptive family to a transracial adoptive
family, the researcher returned the case number of the selected white adopted child

FORM USED FOR COLLECTING THE DATA NEEDED TO MATCH
INTRARACIAL ADOPTIVE FAMILIES TO INTERRACIAL
ADOPTIVE FAMILIES

Black Adoptive Child's Case Number	Birthdate	Last Grade in School Completed by Adoptive Father	Occupation of Adoptive Father (if college student, indicate major field of study)

White Adoptive Child's Case Number	Birthdate	Last Grade in School Completed by Adoptive Father	Occupation of Adoptive Father (if college student, indicate major field of study)
1.			
2.			
3.			
4.			
5.			
6.			
7.			
8.			
9.			
10.			

Agency or Region Office_____   Person filling out form_____

to the agency making the placement. The agencies then sent a letter to the adoptive parents of the selected white children explaining the nature and sponsorship of the project, and asking if they would be willing to share their thoughts about their adoptive experiences with an interviewer. (A sample letter agencies used as a guide in composing the letter to the intraracial adoptive parents is contained in the Appendix.) Along with each letter, the agencies sent a reply card with a self-addressed return envelope to the agency to facilitate the parents' reply.

Step 8): Instructions developed for selecting the study group specified that the adoptive parents of a Black child who indicated an unwillingness to participate were to be eliminated from inclusion in the study group. However, all of the transracial adoptive parents who returned the reply card indicated a willingness to participate.

Also to be eliminated from inclusion in the study group were the adoptive parents of a white child who:

a)   could not be located, or

b)   were unwilling to participate, or

c)   did not reply within three weeks of the mailing date of the letter seeking their participation.

Although most of the intraracial adoptive parents who were contacted indicated a willingness to participate, there were some who checked on the reply card they did not want to participate. There were also several who did not return the reply card (perhaps some may have moved and did not receive the letter from the agency; and others may have received the letter, but were unwilling to participate and therefore did not return the reply card). The exclusion from the study group of a few of these intraracial adoptive parents due to their unwillingness to participate results in some self-selectivity of the comparison group which may have an influence on the findings of the study. The possible effects are discussed in a later chapter.

It would be desirable to know how many intraracial adoptive couples refused to participate. Initially an effort was made to obtain data on refusals. Forms were developed and sent to each agency to use in recording this information. An accurate count, however, was not made for two reasons: a) For the families that did not return the reply card, it was not known if this indicated an unwillingness to participate; or perhaps was due to an oversight in simply forgetting to fill out the reply card; or perhaps due to the family's having moved and not having received the letter. b) The second reason was, as can be seen from the above description, the selection process was already quite complicated and time-consuming for agencies; and therefore it was thought inadvisable to press agencies to fill out an additional form on refusals. Although accurate data on refusals is not available, it is known that a large majority of the intraracial families who were contacted indicated a willingness to participate, and that there were several refusals. (Apparently, white couples who adopt a Black child are more willing to discuss their adoptive experiences than white couples who adopted a child of their own race.)

Every intraracial adoptive family who indicated an unwillingness to participate or who did not return the reply card, was replaced with another intraracial adoptive family. The replacement procedures were as follows. The researcher called each agency every three or four weeks to review the replies. When a replacement was necessary, the researcher selected another family using the information provided by the agency on the form described earlier in Step 4. Agencies then sent a letter to the replacement family inquiring if they were interested in being interviewed about their adoptive experiences. If this family did not indicate a willingness to participate, another family was selected as a replacement using the same procedures.

Step 9): For every adoptive couple indicating a willingness to participate in the project, it was necessary to contact the Judge of the County where the child was adopted to obtain legal permission for: a) the agency to release the names and other identifying information on the adoptive families to the project staff in order that an interview could be arranged and b) the researcher to have access to agency record material on the family. The procedures for obtaining the Judge's permission are as follows. After the agencies received the reply cards from those families willing to participate, the names and other identifying information on these families were sent to the State Division of Family Services. The Division then sent a letter to the Judges of the Counties in which the children were adopted, seeking their permission. Because of the time involved in selecting the study group (seven months); permission was first sought for the transracial group which was selected first; and then a few months later for the intraracial adoptive group following the completion of the selection of these families. (Copies of letters sent to Judges by the Division are included in the Appendix.)

There were 24 counties in the State in which adoptions were finalized for the children in the study group, and the appropriate Judge in each of these counties was sent a letter from the Division seeking their permission. The responses of the Judges were quite favorable. Permission was received from all but one Judge; one white child had been adopted in this County and consequently the adoptive family was excluded from the study group. Three Judges preferred to contact the families in their county by letter to be assured the families were willing to participate, even though the Division indicated in their letter to these Judges that the families already had indicated a willingness to participate.

One Judge required that the adoptive couples sign a consent form giving their permission for the agency to provide their names to the project staff, and giving their permission for the agency to allow the project staff to have access to the agency's record material on the families. Seventeen families in the study group who had previously indicated a willingness to participate in the study adopted a child in this county, and therefore needed to be recontacted for signing the consent form. One of these families (adoptive parents of a white child) did not wish to sign the consent form as they had concerns about allowing the project staff to read the adoptive record material; this family was consequently not included in the study group.

Step 10): After the necessary legal permission was obtained, the Division of Family Services provided the names and other identifying information on the families to the researcher.

Number of Families in Study Group

Through the above mentioned procedures, the names of 48 white families who adopted a Black child were received for inclusion in the study group. This number was very close to the study goal of 50 families for this group. These 48 families probably include almost all of the white couples living in Wisconsin whose adoption of a Black child was finalized prior to March 30, 1970. A couple of considerations lead to this conclusion. First of all, agencies made a concerted effort to contact all of the white families for whom they placed Black children for adoption during the indicated time period, with no refusals being noted. In addition, almost all of the children adopted by unrelated petitioners in the State are agency placements (e.g., in 1968, 97% of such placements were by agencies (Child Welfare Statistics-1968).

It may well be that there are a few other white couples living in Wisconsin whose adoption of a Black child was finalized prior to the end of March 1970; for example, some couples may have adopted a Black child in another state and have since moved to Wisconsin.

Although 48 transracial adoptive families were selected, only 44 were interviewed and thereby considered as composing the transracial study group. Three families were not interviewed because they moved before an interview could be arranged; two moved to a distant state and a third to a foreign country. (It perhaps should be noted several weeks usually transpired between the time when a family consented to be interviewed, and the time when legal permission to contact the family was received.)

A fourth family was not included in the study group because the adoptive father is closely associated with the project; inclusion in the study group was discussed with this adoptive father, and it was mutually agreed that the family should not be included in order to prevent any bias that may have resulted.

For the comparison group, 44 white families who adopted a child of their own race agreed to participate and were matched pair-by-pair to the transracial adoptive families. However, three of these families were later not included in the study group. As indicated earlier, legal permission to include one of these families was not received from the Judge of the county in which the child was adopted. A second family initially indicated a willingness to participate, but when recontacted about signing the consent form, was hesitant to do so as the parents had concerns about the project staff reading the family adoptive record material at the agency. A third family moved before an interview could be arranged.

A total of 44 families was therefore obtained for the transracial adoptive group, and 41 families for the comparison group. Since most statistical tests which have been developed for analyzing data on groups matched on a pair-by-pair basis do not allow for a few subjects to be without a matched pair, the data on the three transracial families who are without a matched intraracial pair will usually not be included in the statistical analysis. However, the data on these three transracial families will usually be included when presenting the results of the study where statistical tests will not be used.

Interviewing of Families and Reading of Adoption Record Material

Copies of the interview schedules for the two groups in the study are included in the Appendix. The interview schedule for the intraracial adoptive families is similar to the schedule for the transracial group, with the major difference being that the racial aspects of the questions were excluded. The interview questions were adapted from interview schedules used in prior adoption studies by Jersild et al. (1949), Edgar, Kadushin (1966), Social Planning Council of Metropolitan Toronto (1966), and by Falk (1968). In addition, consultation assistance in the preparation of the schedules was received from members of the researcher's Doctoral Committee and from interview design specialists at the Wisconsin Survey Research Laboratory.

The interviewing for the project was done by the researcher and four other interviewers. In addition to the researcher, the four other interviewers have extensive training and experience in interviewing for social surveys. Three of the interviewers are employees of the Wisconsin Survey Research Laboratory, and the fourth is an interviewer supervisor for a national survey company. Prior to interviewing families, an orientation meeting was held with the interviewers in which the nature and sponsorship of the study was explained, and in which each question in the schedules was reviewed; clarifying the purpose of the question and indicating when a probe may be appropriate.

The procedures for arranging the interviews are as follows. After the Division of Family Services provided the names and other identifying information on the families in the study group to the researcher, a letter was sent by the researcher to the adoptive parents expressing appreciation for their willingness to participate, and indicating they will soon be called by an interviewer to arrange a convenient time for an interview. (A copy of this letter is in the Appendix; the particular copy in the Appendix was sent to the families who were interviewed by the Wisconsin

Survey Research Lab interviewers.) The letter noted that the interview needed to be held with both parents present; that it was not necessary for the interviewer to talk to the children; and suggested that the families may wish to arrange the interview in a place in their home where it would be relatively private as the interview would focus on their personal experiences.

Following this letter to the adoptive couples, an interviewer telephoned and made arrangements to interview the adoptive parents. Because the study design required both the husband and wife to be interviewed together, almost all of the interviews were held in the evening and on weekends. The length of the interviews ranged from slightly less than one hour to almost three hours. Since there were fewer questions to be asked of the intraracial adoptive families, these interviews tended to be shorter in length.

After the interviewer arrived at the home of the adoptive families and the social introductions had been made, the interviewer used as a guide the following to begin the interview with the transracial adoptive parents:

We want to know what it is like to be adoptive parents, and believe the best way to find out is to talk with parents like yourselves who have adopted a child. Nobody knows as well as you what it is like to be adoptive parents.

Whatever you tell us will be considered confidential. No names will ever be revealed.

In responding to the questions we will be asking, we want you to think primarily in terms of _____ (NAME OF CHILD). When we are referring to _____'s (CHILD) race, may we use the term Negro, or would you prefer we use some other term?

       Other term: _____

A majority of the transracial adoptive parents indicated the term Negro was "O.K." to use, although 13 did indicate they had a preference for "Black." Other terms suggested were mixed race, biracial, colored, dark skin, interracial, and Afro-American.

The introduction of the interviews to the intraracial adoptive couples was identical, except that the last sentence relating to the parents' preference for the term to use in referring to the race of their adopted child was omitted.

It perhaps is important to note the intraracial families were not told before or during the interviews that they were part of a study in which the primary focus was on the experiences of families who adopted a Black child. They were only informed they were participating in a study designed to learn more about the experiences of adoptive families. What they were told is of course true. The reason the purpose of the study was not further specified was because it was thought these intraracial adoptive families may have a tendency to respond to the interview questions in terms of what it might be like to be an adoptive parent of a Black child rather than the desired set of responding in terms of their own intraracial adoptive experiences. That such a concern may have been justified was indicated in an interview with one intraracial adoptive family who had been informed of the more specific focus of the study by a letter received from the Judge of the County in which they adopted a child. (This Judge contacted the family to ask if they were interested in participating in the study before giving his permission for the family to be included in the study group.) This family showed a definite tendency to answer some of the interview questions in terms of what it might be like if they instead had adopted a Black child.

No significant difficulties were encountered by any of the interviewers. The interviewers commented this was one of the most enjoyable surveys they had participated in, which is an indication the interviews went smoothly.

Little needs to be said about the procedures involved in reading the record material on the adoptive families. A copy of the record schedule used in gathering information is contained in the Appendix. This schedule was developed with consultation assistance from members of the researcher's Doctoral Committee. The records were read by the researcher at the adoption agencies. For the adoptive families who were selected by the Regional Offices of the State Division of Family Services; the family records are kept at the Regional Offices and were read there, while the records on the children are kept at the central office for the State and were read there. Most of the items for which information was gathered from the record material were objective; e.g., age, religion, education, length of time married, and occupation of adoptive parents at time of placement. Since interpretation and categorization of the information collected from the record material were limited, a reliability check of the accuracy with which the data were taken from the records was not made.

CHAPTER III

CHARACTERISTICS OF ADOPTIVE FAMILIES

Review of Prior Studies

Several studies have investigated differences in personality characteristics, attitudes, and social attributes between parents who adopted a child of their own race (intraracial; IRA parents) and those who adopted a Black child (transracial; TRA parents).[*]

Although TRA couples have been found to be represented along the whole socio-economic spectrum, they tend to have a higher socio-economic status than IRA couples (Roskies, 1963; Shepherd, 1964; Lebo et al., 1965; Falk, 1968; Granger, 1969; and St. Denis, 1969). TRA couples have also been found to participate in activities with friends more frequently than IRA couples (Lebo, et al., 1965).

In a descriptive study of 21 white couples who adopted a Black child, the Social Planning Council of Metropolitan Toronto (1966) found certain preconceptions about TRA couples are inaccurate. The study group families were not unsociable in the sense of isolating themselves from the surrounding community. In addition, their social contacts were not unusually cosmopolitan, nor were they particularly active in organizations to promote causes.

Marmor (1964) suggests TRA parents tend to be unusually free from tendencies toward ethnocentrism. Marmor states,

> By "ethnocentrism" is meant the tendency to think in relatively rigid ingroup terms, with superior values being attributed to the ingroup and inferior ones to the outgroups--

> In contrast, the nonethnocentric person does not tend to think in terms of ingroup-outgroup hierarchies, but rather to evaluate people on their objective merits as human beings regardless of race, religion, or other group identifications. (pp. 5-6)

Being relatively free of ethnocentrism tendencies, Marmor proceeds to deduce TRA parents are likely to be emotionally mature, to have a large capacity for frustration tolerance, and to be independent thinkers who have a minimal need to rely on family or community approval for their activities.

St. Denis (1969) hypothesized and found TRA fathers have a higher self-concept than IRA fathers, and TRA mothers possess more liberal child-rearing attitudes than IRA mothers. The study group consisted of 147 couples and 2 single women who adopted a Black child, and a randomly selected comparison group of 103 IRA couples.

In an extensive study using a mailed questionnaire, Falk (1968 and 1970) compared certain characteristics and attitudes of 186 transracial adoptive couples to 170 intraracial adoptive couples. The adopted children of the transracial parents in this

---

[*]Note: Although other types of transracial placements have been made (such as Indian and Oriental children with white families) the symbol "TRA" in this study will only be used to refer to white parents who adopted a Black child.

study were of various races; 73 were of Black ancestry, 111 of Indian ancestry, 8 of Oriental ancestry, and 13 were classified as "other mixed" (1970, p. 84). The transracial adoptive couples were found to be more distant geographically and socially from their friends and relatives; tended to be more active in community voluntary organizations; to have been married longer at the time of adoption, and more likely to have genetic children. In turning to the expressed reasons for adopting, the transracial parents were more likely to report having adopted for humanitarian reasons as compared to intraracial parents who more frequently stated they adopted in order to have a child or an additional child.

In a study of 17 TRA couples using agency records, Granger (1969) found only a few TRA parents have close daily contacts with Blacks, but many report having had close contact at some time in the past. Almost three-fourths (12) of the fathers were employed in fields primarily involving close contact with people. The parents tended to be concerned about social problems, but few were actively involved in Civil Rights activities. The primary motivation to adopt was described as "the desire to share the love and security of their family with a child who might not otherwise experience this" (p. 7). The characteristics of these TRA parents are summarized as being:

> Altogether, they are highly intelligent, flexible, and capable people who
> seem to place greater value on the quality and purpose of life than the
> material. In many ways, they have the temperament needed to stand up to
> their families and community, if need be, in becoming parents to these
> children, and the strength of purpose to weather the storm if it comes ...
> In the main, people who apply for transracial adoption are well-adjusted
> people with a happy home life and good marriages. Their motivation most
> usually seems to spring from a deep concern over social problems and a
> strong desire to give of themselves to a child who might not otherwise have
> parents because of existing conditions. (p. 9)

The Question of Marginal Eligibility

Kadushin (1962) found adoptive parents of hard-to-place children are more likely at the time of adoption to have marginal eligibility for adoptive parenthood. The study compared the eligibility status of 91 couples adopting hard-to-place children to the eligibility status of 91 adoptive couples of healthy, normal, white infants. Age (at least one of the spouses over 40) was found to be the most frequent barrier to full eligibility for adoptive parents of hard-to-place children. These adoptive parents also had more health problems; more divorces in the past; more mixed marriages (spouses being members of different religions or races); and a greater number had two or more children in the home. In addition, although the differences were not statistically significant, these adoptive parents tended to have completed four years of school, and to have a lower occupational status than adoptive parents of healthy, white infants.

The hard-to-place children in the study group were either physically or mentally handicapped, over age six at the time of placement, or members of a racial minority. At the time in which the study was conducted, few if any adoption agencies in the state (Wisconsin) were placing Black children with white families; therefore, it is doubtful Black children were in the study group.

The reason advanced by Kadushin for these findings is that marginal eligibility applicants, aware of their eligibility status, believe it is somewhat unlikely the agency will offer a "normal" child for adoption, and therefore compensate for their marginal eligibility by accepting a child with special needs.

Kadushin's findings suggest white parents who adopt Black children may also have marginal eligibility. Such a deduction, however, has been questioned by studies which have found white adoptive parents of Black children tend to have a higher, rather than lower, socio-economic status than adoptive parents of white children (Roskies, 1963; Shepherd, 1964; Lebo et al., 1965; Falk, 1968; and St. Denis, 1969). As will be indicated in the next section, the education and occupation levels of the TRA families in this study are also high.

The socio-economic status of adoptive parents, however, is only one of numerous factors considered by adoption agencies in assessing an applicant's eligibility for adoptive parenthood. Since the marginal eligibility question has been raised, it was thought worthwhile to more closely examine this area with the present study data. If TRA parents generally have marginal eligibility, such parents may be less likely to provide the adopted child with a permanent, stable family experience. Pringle (1967) is quite critical of the practice (if it exists) of agencies placing hard-to-place children with adopters who are more apt to have marginal eligibility:

> If this practice were found to be widespread, its desirability is questionable on practical as well as on ethical grounds. Indeed, it could be argued that handicapped babies need acceptance and the security of a family life even more than normal ones. (p. 28)

It is of course not possible in this study to compare differences in eligibility for adoption due to socio-economic status between the TRA group and the IRA group, since the two groups were matched on occupation and education. The two groups can, however, be compared on the extent to which they possess other eligibility factors that serve as barriers to adoptive placement. Before presenting such data, a word of caution about generalizing the results needs to be made. As noted earlier, the IRA couples were not randomly selected, but were matched to the TRA group on socio-economic level. Because of this matching, the socio-economic level of the IRA couples in the study group is probably higher than the average socio-economic status of white parents who adopt a child of their own race. What effect this selectivity on socio-economic status for the IRA group may have on other eligibility factors for adoptive parenthood is not known, but generalizations should probably not be made to intra-racial adoptive families having a different socio-economic status.

The marginal eligibility criteria used in Kadushin's study (1962) will also be used in this study. Kadushin examined five eligibility factors identified by Schapiro (1956) as being the most common barriers to adoptive parenthood. These five factors are: 1) At least one of the spouses is over 40 years of age; 2) The spouses are members of different religions or races; 3) At least one of the spouses has been divorced; 4) There is a health problem; and 5) There are two or more children in the home. Data on these factors were gathered in this study from the adoption record material and are presented in Table 3.

Since psychodynamic factors are also used by agencies to evaluate an applicant's eligibility, data were also gathered from the record material on two rather broad psychodynamic categories; 1) Questionable personality characteristics for adoptive parenthood, and 2) Problematic areas in life situation, such as problems in the areas of sexual adjustment, marital relationship, in-law relations, adjustment to infertility, and relationships with children in the family. It should be noted such psychodynamic factors cannot be assessed with the same degree of precision as for the factors identified by Schapiro. In assessing whether such psychodynamic factors are problems, human judgments are made, first by the social worker, and then by the reader of the record. Although the validity of the data is not above question, it was thought

Table 3

FREQUENCY OF ELIGIBILITY BARRIERS AMONG TRA COUPLES AND IRA COUPLES

Eligibility Barriers	Frequency	
	TRA Couples (N = 41)	IRA Couples (N = 41)
Over 40	6	7
Mixed marriage	2	5
History of divorce	1	1
Health problems	2	2
Two or more children in the home	25	7
Questionable personality characteristics	4	4
Problematic areas in life situation	6	7

such data would provide additional information about the adopters' eligibility status at the time of the adoptive home study.

Table 3 shows the only notable difference in frequency of eligibility barriers is that TRA families are substantially more likely to have two or more children in the home. However, it is questionable whether having two or more children can be considered as an eligibility barrier. Since Schapiro's study in 1956, agencies have relaxed the guideline that prospective adoptive couples should be infertile, and therefore are unlikely to view having a couple of children in the home as being an eligibility barrier (Child Welfare League of America, 1968). The revised policy guidelines of the Child Welfare League of America (1968) for placing children with parents who have other children are:

Preference should not be given to couples who are childless. (p. 52)

Families with natural or adopted children should be given the same consideration as childless couples. (p. 52)

An additional reason for excluding this factor is that TRA parents are also unlikely to perceive having children in the home as being a barrier. (The perception of possessing an eligibility barrier plays a key part in Kadushin's (1962) explanation of why applicants with marginal eligibility are more apt to adopt a hard-to-place child.) As will be expanded upon in a later section, TRA couples do not tend to adopt a Black child as a second-choice to a white child; but appear to adopt because they believe they have "room for one more" child who otherwise may not be adopted.

If the factor regarding the number of children in the home is excluded from the analysis, it can be concluded from Table 3: on the factors examined, TRA couples do not show a higher frequency of eligibility barriers than the IRA couples.

As indicated previously, generalization of this finding is limited because IRA couples were not randomly selected, but matched to TRA couples on socio-economic status.

23

However, since the same eligibility factors were used in Kadushin's (1962) study, it is possible to compare the data on the TRA couples in this study to the two groups in Kadushin's study; one group adopted hard-to-place children (but probably Black children were not included), and the other randomly selected group adopted healthy, normal, white infants.

Using a standard score test for differences between proportions of two samples, TRA couples were significantly more likely than the other two groups to have two or more children in the home. However, if this factor is excluded from consideration for the reasons previously described, the TRA couples do not differ significantly from adoptive couples of normal, white infants on the other four eligibility barriers; in fact, on three of the four factors a slightly lower proportion of TRA couples possess the barrier.

Table 4

ELIGIBILITY BARRIERS AMONG: TRA COUPLES; ADOPTIVE COUPLES OF OTHER HARD-TO-PLACE CHILDREN; AND ADOPTIVE COUPLES OF NORMAL, WHITE INFANTS

| | Frequency and Percent | | | | | |
| | Adoptive Couples of Normal, White Infants (N = 91, Kadushin's data, 1962) | | TRA Couples (N = 41) | | Adoptive Couples of Hard-to-Place Children (N = 91, Kadushin's data, 1962) | |
Eligibility Barriers	No.	%	No.	%	No.	%
Over 40	18	20	6	15	87	96 *
Mixed marriage	5	6	2	5	15	17
History of divorce	7	8	1	2	12	13
Health problem	4	4	2	5	7	8
Two or more children in the home	2	2 *	25	61	6	7 *

Note: The results of the Z test for data shown on Table 4 are presented in Appendix L.

* Standard score test (two-tailed, 0.5 level) found a significant difference between this percentage and the percentage for TRA couples on the comparable item.

In comparing the results between the TRA couples and the adoptive couples of hard-to-place children, it is noted the latter group of couples is significantly more likely to have at least one of the spouses over 40 years of age. In addition, on two other items, "mixed marriage" and "history of divorce," the difference approached significance (if a one-tailed test had been used, the hard-to-place group would have been found to be significantly more likely to also possess these eligibility barriers).

Thus, in reference to the question of marginal eligibility, it appears white adoptive parents of a Black child are as eligible for adoption parenthood as couples who adopt normal, white infants.

Equally interesting, TRA couples apparently are less likely than adoptive couples of hard-to-place children other than Black, to have marginal eligibility for adoptive parenthood. This difference leads to the conjecture that TRA couples may differ substantially from adoptive couples of other types of hard-to-place children on other variables; e.g., on personality characteristics, social attributes, and attitudes. An investigation into such possible differences is beyond the scope of this project.

There are, however, findings from other studies which lend support to this conjecture. TRA couples tend, as indicated earlier, to have a high socio-economic status, while adoptive parents of other hard-to-place children have been found by Mass (1960) and Kadushin (1962) to have a somewhat lower socio-economic status.

Falk (1968) compared the questionnaire responses between white couples who adopted a Black child and white couples who adopted an Indian child. On most items no significant differences were found. However, there were a few important differences. The two groups differed on occupational status, with a larger proportion of couples who adopted an Indian child being farmers. Also the couples who adopted an Indian child were less likely to say they adopted because of the child's needs, and also more likely to indicate that it is more difficult to rear a Black child than an Indian child.

A difference in characteristics is also suggested in Fanshel's (1966) study of white couples who adopted an Indian child. The motivation for adopting appeared to be similar to intraracial adoptive parents in that they wanted a child (and not specifically an Indian child), and it was noted they did not appear to be particularly motivated by social consciousness or humanitarian reasons. Fanshel also asked if they would have considered adopting a Black child when they applied for adoption and found,

> Of utmost interest is the finding that despite the fact that these families had already adopted children who are, in most cases, easily recognizable as being in a minority ethnic group, they almost uniformly felt that they could not undertake to adopt a child of mixed Black-white parentage. This was their response even for a child who is described as not obviously Black in appearance. (p. 12)

These parents were quite apologetic about their unwillingness to consider adopting a Black child, and explained they felt their communities were not as yet ready to accept the adoption of a Black child. Such a feeling, of course, suggests additudinal differences between these parents and those who are willing to adopt a Black child.

Identifying Data on Adoptive Parents

A. Socio-Economic Status: As indicated earlier, one of the notable characteristics of TRA parents is they generally have a high socio-economic status. As described in the previous chapter, IRA families were matched pair-by-pair to TRA families on the occupation and education of the adoptive father. Warner's Occupation Scale (Miller, 1964) which is presented in the Appendix was used to rank the occupation of the adoptive fathers. Table 5 presents the distribution of the occupational rankings at the time of adoptive placement.

The rankings tend to be concentrated in the first two levels, which primarily include professional people; and proprietors, executives, and managers of businesses.

Table 5

OCCUPATIONAL RANKINGS OF ADOPTIVE FATHERS AT TIME OF PLACEMENT

Occupational Level	TRA Fathers (N = 41)		IRA Fathers (N = 41)	
	No.	%	No.	%
1	19	46	17	42
2	13	32	9	22
3	3	7	7	17
4	1	2	4	10
5	4	10	3	7
6	1	2	1	2
7				
Totals	41	99	41	100

Table 6 shows the distribution of the number of school years completed by the parents in the study group at time of adoption. As shown in Table 6, the educational level achieved by these adoptive parents is high. Only 6 (4%) did not graduate from high school, and 90 (55%) graduated from college, with a number receiving advanced degrees.

Considering only the TRA parents, the data indicates the educational level is substantially higher than the average level achieved by the general population (the 1960 Census found the median school years completed by Wisconsin residents age 25 and over is 10.4 years). Gardner (1969) also found the TRA parents in his study tended to have a college education. In commenting on this association, Gardner notes,

> ... it would appear that education and perhaps, also being exposed to different philosophies and persons of different backgrounds while attending school, is related to one's ability to accept a child of another race as one's own. (p. 2)

It should be noted, however, it would be a mistake to stereotype TRA parents as being college education; the range of school years completed by TRA parents in this study was from the 8th grade through receiving a doctorate, with 22 (27%) never having attended college or vocational school.

B. Age of Adoptive Couples: In a study on transracial adoptions, St. Denis (1969) found the TRA parents in his study group tended to be slightly older than a randomly selected control group of white couples who adopted a child of their own race.

Table 7 presents the distribution of the ages of the adoptive fathers in this study at the time of placement. The ages of the TRA fathers ranged from 24 to 47 years with a mean of 33.7 years. The ages of the IRA fathers ranged from 25 to 47 years, with a mean of 33.8 years. A Wilcoxon matched-pairs signed-ranks test for age differences between the two groups was not significant.

The distribution of the ages of the adoptive mothers at time of placement is presented in Table 8. The ages of the TRA mothers ranged from 23 to 43 years, with a mean of 31.0 years; while the age range for the IRA mothers was from 24 to 47 years,

Table 6

YEARS EDUCATION COMPLETED BY ADOPTIVE PARENTS AT TIME OF PLACEMENT

Education Completed	TRA Fathers		IRA Fathers		TRA Mothers		IRA Mothers	
	No.	%	No.	%	No.	%	No.	%
Through 8th grade					1	2		
H.S. (but not graduate)	1	2	1	2	2	5	1	2
H.S. graduate	9	22	8	20	9	22	13	32
College (but not graduate) or vocational training following H.S.	5	12	8	20	6	15	10	24
Four-year college graduate	7	17	11	27	17	42	13	32
Advanced degree graduate	19	46	13	32	6	15	4	10
Totals	41	99	41	101	41	101	41	101

Table 7

AGES OF ADOPTIVE FATHERS AT TIME OF PLACEMENT

Age in Years	TRA Fathers	IRA Fathers
20-24	2	0
25-29	7	8
30-34	14	16
35-39	12	11
40-44	5	5
45-49	1	1
Totals	41	41

Note: The results of Wilcoxon matched-pairs signed-ranks tests for data shown on Tables 7, 8, 9, and 16 are presented in Appendix M.

Table 8

AGES OF ADOPTIVE MOTHERS AT TIME OF PLACEMENT

Age in Years	TRA Mothers	IRA Mothers
20-24	3	2
25-29	14	20
30-34	16	10
35-39	3	8
40-44	5	0
45-49	0	1
Totals	41	41

with a mean of 30.5 years. A Wilcoxon matched-pairs signed-ranks test for age differences between the two groups was not significant.

This study's findings of insignificant age differences between TRA and IRA parents are inconsistent with St. Denis' (1969) results which found the TRA fathers and mothers in his study were significantly older at the time of placement. One explanation for this discrepancy is related to the matching on socio-economic level. In St. Denis' study, the IRA parents were randomly selected, while in this study they were matched to the TRA parents on occupation and education. As indicated earlier, such matching probably led to a higher average socio-economic level among the IRA parents in this study than is characteristic of the general population of white adotive parents of a white child. Intraracial parents who have a high socio-economic status may tend to adopt at an older age; e.g., they may prefer to complete college and become financially secure before applying to adopt.

C.   Number of Years Married: The number of years married at time of placement for the TRA couples ranged from 1 to 22 years, with a mean of 9.5 years. The number of years married for the IRA couples ranged from 1 year to 14 years, with a mean of 6.9 years. Table 9 presents the distribution of the number of years married. A Wilcoxon matched-pairs signed-ranks test for differences in number of years married between the two groups was significant (two-tailed, .05 level).

Table 9

NUMBER OF YEARS MARRIED AT TIME OF PLACEMENT

Length of Marriage in Years	TRA Couples	IRA Couples
0-3	2	3
4-6	9	19
7-9	13	11
10-12	7	6
13-15	6	2
16-18	2	
19-21	1	
22-25	1	
Totals	41	41

St. Denis (1969) also found transracial adoptive parents were married longer than intraracial adoptive parents at time of placement.

D.   Location of Adoptive Couples: Using the 1970 Census data, the population of the communities in which the families were located was identified, with the distribution of the results presented in Table 10. For cities with suburbs, the size of community includes the population of the city and surrounding suburbs.

The data show TRA families tend to reside in larger urban communities. In fact, 25 (61%) of the TRA families were located in the two largest metropolitan areas of the state (Madison and Milwaukee).

E.   Presence of Other Adopted Children: Some study group families have adopted other children in addition to the children selected for the study. Table 11 presents

28

Table 10

LOCATION OF ADOPTIVE COUPLES AT TIME OF FOLLOW-UP INTERVIEW

Population of Community	TRA Families	IRA Families
Rural	5	4
5,000	1	10
5,000-25,000	3	3
25,000-75,000	3	2
75,000-150,000	3	6
150,000	26	16
Totals	41	41

Table 11

NUMBER OF OTHER ADOPTED CHILDREN IN FAMILIES
AT TIME OF FOLLOW-UP INTERVIEW

Number of Children	TRA Families	IRA Families
0	24	24
1	13	15
2	2	2
3		
4	1	
5	1	
Totals	41	41

the distribution of the number of other children adopted by TRA and IRA couples at the time of the follow-up interview.

The results are similar for the two groups; 24 families (59%) in both groups have not adopted another child. Of the 26 "other" adopted children by TRA families, 20 are transracial placements; 8 of Black ancestry, 7 of Korean ancestry, and 5 of Indian ancestry.

Reasons for Adopting

Harriet Fricke (1965) categorizes adoptive applicants into two types: "traditional," applicants for healthy, normal, white infants; and "room-for-one-more," applicants for children of another race. Miss Fricke writes:

By virtue of their infertility, traditional applicants wish to adopt because they need children. Furthermore, because they are denied the satisfaction of reproducing themselves, these couples wish to adopt children similar to themselves; minimally this includes the desire to adopt children of their own race.

Finally, because traditional applicants must depend upon agencies to achieve parenthood, they approach agencies with a hat-in-hand attitude, tending to bend over backward not to jeopardize their opportunity for adoption.

Conversely, "room-for-one-more" applicants, by virtue of their fertility, wish to adopt because they know children need them. And since they have had and can have the satisfaction of reproducing themselves, these applicants comfortably can encompass adopting children different from themselves, including youngsters of another race. Last, but certainly not least, these applicants do not approach adoption workers obsequiously. They come to offer, not beg. (p. 5)

Although such a categorization may be an over-simplification of the characteristics and motivations of transracial and intraracial adoptive parents, data in this study lend support to Fricke's "ideal" types.

Deductions from Fricke's categories suggest TRA couples are more likely to be fertile and more apt to have natural-born children. Tables 12 and 13 support such deductions. Of the TRA couples, 33 (80%) were known to be fertile at the time of placement, compared to only 11 (27%) IRA couples. In addition, at time of placement, only 6 (15%) of the TRA couples did not have genetic children, as compared to 26 (63%) of the IRA couples. These differences between the two study groups appear to be important. As Fricke suggests, such differences are probably related to the TRA couples' interest in adopting a hard-to-place child, and (as will be presented and discussed later) may also account for some of the differences between the two study groups in satisfactions derived from the adoptive experience.

Table 12

CAPABILITY FOR NATURAL PARENTHOOD AT TIME OF PLACEMENT

Fertility Status	TRA Couples		IRA Couples	
	No.	%	No.	%
Fertile	33	81	11	27
Infertile	6	15	18	44
Infertility unclear, but failure to conceive	2	5	12	29
Totals	41	101	41	100

Table 13

NUMBER OF GENETIC CHILDREN IN FAMILIES AT TIME OF PLACEMENT

Number of Genetic Children	TRA Families (N = 41)	IRA Families (N = 41)
0	6	26
1	12	9
2	3	2
3	5	2
4	3	2
5	9	
6	1	
7	1	
8	1	
Total Number of Genetic Children	111	27

30

Another notable feature of Table 13 is that TRA couples are not only more likely to have genetic children, but also more apt to have a larger number of genetic children. Fifteen (37%) of the TRA couples had four or more genetic children at time of placement, compared to only 2 (5%) of the IRA couples. Such a difference may be related (as Fricke suggests) to TRA couples being more motivated to adopt because of the child's need for a family, and also to their desire to include within their family a child of another race. In addition, because there tends to be an oversupply of adoptive applicants for white, normal infants, adoptive agencies may be somewhat more hesitant to place white, normal infants with applicants who already have a large number of genetic children.

The reasons expressed by couples for adopting also lend support to Fricke's categories. These reasons are presented in Table 14. Data on these reasons were gathered from the interviews and from the record material. During the interview the TRA couples and IRA couples were asked:

Thinking of the time prior to your adopting _____ (CHILD) can you tell me the reasons why you were considering adopting?

An additional question only asked of TRA couples was:

What were your reasons for deciding to adopt a Black child?

In examining Table 14, most of the expressed reasons for adopting appear to be "healthy," with a few appearing questionable or even "unhealthy"; e.g., "fill void left by deceased child," "lonely without children," and "adopting a Black child is a challenge." In regard to these latter reasons, it should be noted these phrases are taken out of context; and that such questionable reasons tended to be given towards the end of a series of reasons presented by the adoptive parents. When presented by the adoptive parents, less pathology seemed indicated than when the reasons are displayed individually.

In reviewing the reasons for adopting, it appears IRA families tend to adopt for parent-centered reasons; they want children to fulfill their life and marriage, to complete their family, to be a companion for other children in their family, and a majority indicate they wish to adopt because they are unable to have natural-born children. This last reason mentioned for adopting suggests a tendency on their part to view adoption as a second-choice method to enlarging their family.

The reasons expressed by TRA families, on the other hand, tend to be child-centered; primarily to provide a home to a child who otherwise may not be adopted. As indicated earlier, these couples generally are able to bear children; but because of the need for adoptive homes, tend to view adopting a Black child as being the first-choice method to enlarging their family. Their attitude is apparently typified in the following comment by a TRA parent, "I think we could have more children of our own, but we thought with so many children without a home we would try to give one of them a home."

TRA families also appear to be concerned about social issues as indicated by two of their reasons for adopting; "To further human relations (integration)" and "Concerns about over-population." Although many of these families during the interviews expressed rather strong feelings about racial inequalities in our society, the adoption records indicated only a small minority (eight couples--20%) were actively involved in civil rights activities; and among those families involved in civil rights activities, no incidents of militant civil rights activity were noted in the record

Table 14

ADOPTERS' EXPRESSED REASONS FOR ADOPTING CHILD

	Frequency	
Reason	TRA Couples (N = 41)	IRA Couples (N = 41)
Desire for (more) children or specific sex child	21	37
Provide a home to a child who otherwise may not be adopted	36	2
Are unable to have natural-born children	--	27
Further human relations (integration)	14	--
Want companion for other child(ren) in family	6	11
Fulfill life and marriage--to complete family	--	12
Concern about over-population	11	--
Believe are able to provide a good home to a child	9	3
Enjoy children	6	3
Have had personal experiences and formed positive relationships with Blacks which adds to belief that the outcome of adopting a Black (part-Black) child will be successful	7	--
Adoption agency mentioned need to find adoptive parents for Black and mixed-Black children	6	--
Want a family of adopted and natural born children	5	1
Child was a foster child in our home and we became attached to	5	1
Religious convictions (Lord has blessed us, we should help others in need)	4	2
Feel are able to love a Black (or racially mixed) child as well as children born to us	5	--
Articles in newspapers and church bulletins described need for adoptive homes of children with Black ancestry	4	--
Have friends who adopted a mixed-Black child with a successful outcome	3	--
Want a family of different races and nationalities	3	--
Adopting a Black or part-Black child will facilitate the development of attitudes of brotherhood and tolerance in our other children	3	--
Children are children, color of skin makes no difference to us	2	--
Adopting a Black (part-Black) child is a way to live our beliefs	2	--
Adopting a Black child is a challenge	2	--
Will help other child in family learn to share	--	2
Relatives adopted children with a successful outcome	--	2
Had foster children so knew we could love and accept a child who was not born to us	--	2
Lonely without children	1	1
Fill void left by deceased child	1	1
Exciting to watch children develop	--	1
Totals	156	108

material. (Perhaps it should be noted that while the 20% figure for involvement in civil rights activities appears to be a small percentage, this percentage may be larger than the percent of the white population in this country who are actively involved in civil rights activities.) The following summary comments about three TRA couples by adoption workers in the record material appear to typify these families:

(a) "They are not do-gooders or activists in terms of civil rights or equality, but their sympathies lie with such concerns."

(b) "Their motivation in wanting a mixed-racial child is a part of them and their way of life rather than a social cause ... they would not exploit a child in the cause of civil rights."

(c) "They feel they are somehow lessening the gap between isolation of the races and the integration of the races in this country, but do not consider their adopted child or themselves as showpieces."

It is interesting to note such laudatory comments do not appear in the record material of white couples who were among the first to apply for a Black child several years ago. Originally, adoption agencies appeared to be highly suspicious of the motivations of couples who expressed an interest in adopting a Black child, and frequently the agencies sought psychiatric consultations on such cases. The following comments recorded in an adoption record several years ago indicate the suspicious reactions of one adoption worker to the first family to apply for a Black child at the agency:

I know very little of their own background, but I feel that probably both of them are basically rebellious people and this request for a child of mixed race is a manifestation of this great rebellion. As far as motivation is concerned, I felt that it was very strong and also very sick. The _____ (applying couple) talk a lot about "equality," and in a pretty starry-eyed and idealistic way feel that they want to have a part in promoting the brotherhood of man.

Two-mixed Black children were later placed with this family, with the record material indicating the agency is pleased with the outcome. Inclusion of such a comment is not meant to be a criticism of agencies, but a statement about the history of transracial placements. Agencies justifiably need to be cautious and carefully assess new programs which will have a substantial effect on the children who receive services.

After beginning to place Black children with such couples, agencies have become more accepting (in fact, encouraging) of transracial placements. (Conversations with adoption workers indicate, however, some workers still question or disapprove of Black-white adoptions.) Apparently, as also happened in some other states (Fricke, 1965; Issac, 1965) the white parents who first applied for Black children played an important role in stimulating agencies to make transracial placements.

Reservations at Time of Adopting

One of the questions asked during the interview was:

What reservations did you have at the time when you were considering adopting _____ (CHILD)?

The responses are presented in Table 15.

Table 15

RESERVATIONS WHEN CONSIDERING ADOPTING

Concerns	TRA Couples (N = 41)	IRA Couples (N = 41)
None	8	25
Reactions of relatives and if would accept child	11	2
Reactions of community and if would accept child	9	--
Identity development of non-white child in white family	9	--
Effects of adoption on genetic children	7	--
Capacity to love adopted child as much as genetic	1	6
Financial	5	1
Capacity to care for another child	4	--
Reactions of child to being raised in a white community	4	--
Personality and physical appearance of child when older (when is an adolescent or an adult)	2	2
Effects of adopting a Black child on adoptive parents	3	--
Limitations on family mobility (traveling and place of residence) due to adopting a Black child	3	--
Physical appearance of child	1	2
Heredity background and health of child	--	2
Reactions of neighbors and if would accept child	2	--
Problems due to race that may develop, and parental ability to cope with	2	--
Loss of public anonymity due to visual physical difference of child	1	--
As child grows older, will he wonder about the motives of his white parents in adopting him	1	--
Nature of racial problems in future years	1	--
Will child be rejected by both white and black races	1	--
How to tell child he is adopted	--	1
Stigma that might be attached to child due to adoptive status	--	1
How to take care of a baby	--	1
How involved adoption procedures will be	--	1

As might be expected, TRA families had more concerns at the time of adoption, with most of their concerns centering around problems that may develop in adopting a child of another race.

During the interview the IRA families were asked if they had considered adopting a child of some other race besides white; 12 of the families indicated they had considered adopting a nonwhite child, with 8 of these families mentioning they had considered adopting a Black (or mixed-Black child). The reasons given for not adopting a Black child were: concern over acceptance of child by relatives and community; agency did not encourage a mixed-race placement, wanted first child to be white; thought problems would develop and were uncertain if would be able to handle; and "did not have enough courage."

Identifying Data on Adoptive Children

Of the adopted children in the TRA group, 18 are boys and 23 are girls; the reverse is the case for the IRA group, 23 are boys and 18 are girls. All the children except one were separated from the natural parents shortly after birth; one child, a white child, was removed from the natural mother at 4 months of age due to abuse and neglect.

Table 16 shows the distribution of the ages of the children at time of adoptive placement. The ages of the TRA children at time of placement ranged from less than a month to 35 months; for the IRA group the range is from less than a month to 25 months. The mean age at time of placement for the TRA group was 6.0 months, and the mean for the IRA group was 3.8 months. A Wilcoxon matched pairs signed-ranks test for age differences at time of placement between the two groups was not significant (two-tailed, .05 level); the age differences, however, approached significance, a one-tailed test would have been significant.

Table 16

AGES OF ADOPTED CHILDREN AT TIME OF PLACEMENT

Age in Months	TRA Group	IRA Group
3	15	27
3-5	12	9
6-9	3	1
10-12	3	--
13-15	4	1
16-18	1	2
19-21	1	--
22-24	1	--
24	1	1
Totals	41	41

The distribution of the number of foster home placements for the two groups is presented in Table 17. The two groups are very similar on this item, with most of the children in both groups having had one foster home placement prior to being placed with their adoption parents.

An effort was made to gather data from the record material on the types of behavioral problems manifested by these children prior to adoptive placement. Very few problems were noted, probably because most of the children were still infants when

Table 17

NUMBER OF FOSTER HOME PLACEMENTS PRIOR TO PLACEMENT IN ADOPTIVE HOME

Number of Foster Home Placements	TRA Children	IRA Children
0	3	1
1	30	32
2	6	5
3	2	1
Totals	41	41

placed for adoption. The only child for whom some concern was expressed in the record material was the white child mentioned earlier who had been removed from an abusive and neglectful mother at 4 months of age. Prior to being placed for adoption this child was described as being unresponsive to affection, fearful at times, and somewhat slow in developing. Following placement with the adoptive parents, the record indicates the child made "rapid strides," and by the time the adoption was finalized, the record indicates the agency was satisfied with the child's emotional development.

Information was also gathered from the record material on serious health problems prior to adoptive placement. No chronic health problems were noted for the Black children in the study. However, five of the white children had rather serious medical problems. One was born with a cleft palate, another had a heart defect requiring open heart surgery, and a third was born with leg deformities which required extensive orthopedic treatment. A fourth child was born with three extra sets of ribs and vertebrae and a double colon; while the fifth child, although healthy, had an ancestry in which Huntington's Chorea was present on the natural mother's side.

Table 18 shows the distribution of the ages of the children at the time of the follow-up interview. The age range for the TRA children is from 19 months to 67

Table 18

AGES OF CHILDREN AT TIME OF FOLLOW-UP INTERVIEW

Age in Years	TRA Children	IRA Children
1.5-2.0	11	10
2.0-2.5	9	10
2.5-3.0	5	4
3.0-3.5	4	7
3.5-4.0	4	1
4.0-4.5	2	3
4.5-5.0	2	2
5.0-5.5	3	--
5.5-6.0	1	3
6.0-6.5	--	1
Totals	41	41

months, with a mean of 34.8 months. For the IRA children the age range is from 19 months to 73 months, with a mean of 35.7 months. Since the children in the two groups were matched pair-by-pair on age it is not surprising that the mean ages at time of follow-up interview are similar for the two groups. The slight difference between mean ages for the two groups is probably due to the highly involved selection process for the study group (as described in the previous chapter) which resulted in the IRA families being selected and interviewed a few weeks after the TRA families.

The average lapse of time between placement and follow-up interview can be obtained by comparing the mean age at follow-up interview to the mean age at time of placement. The average lapse of time for the TRA group was 28.8 months (34.8 months at follow-up - 6.0 months at placement). For the IRA group the average lapse was 32.9 months (35.7 months at follow-up - 3.8 months at placement).

An effort was made to determine the "racial" composition of the TRA children from information in the record material. As indicated previously, there are no clearly delineating , biological classifications of races, and usually in social research a social definition of race is used; e.g., anyone having any known Black ancestry (see e.g., Rose, 1964; Pettigrew, 1964; and Berry, 1965).

One of the standard items in adoption records is the race of the natural mother and of the natural father. Frequently adoption agencies do not have contact with the alleged father, and need to rely on the natural mother (usually unwed) for a description of his race and other characteristics. Although the chance of error exists due to the inexact science of racial categorization, the distribution of the races of the natural parents as recorded in the records is presented in Table 19.

Table 19

RACE OF NATURAL PARENTS OF TRA CHILDREN

Race of Natural Parents	Number of TRA Children
White mother = part-Black father	7
White mother = Black father	29
Indian mother = Black father	1
Part-Black mother = part-Black father	1
Part-Black mother = Black father	1
Black mother = part-Black father	1
Black mother = Black father	1
Total	41

According to the information in Table 19, 40 of the 41 TRA children can be considered to have "mixed-Black" parentage, while only one has "all-Black" parentage. Interestingly, 36 (88%) of the natural mothers were white, while all of the natural fathers were Black (or part-Black). The reasons for this phenomenon are known; it may partially be due to the greater tendency of Black mothers may also be more likely to place their part-Black babies for adoption in an effort to conceal the out-of-wedlock birth, and to avoid the social stigma of being recognized as becoming illegitimately impregnated by a Black.

CHAPTER IV

EXPERIENCES OF TRANSRACIAL AND INTRARACIAL ADOPTIVE FAMILIES

Feeling of Being a Parent To Child

During the interview the parents were asked:

Do you feel, now, that _____ (CHILD) is really your own child?

All of the respondents in both groups replied affirmatively. The parents were then asked:

How long after _____ (CHILD) was placed with you did it take before you felt he/she was really your own? (Both spouses were requested to respond)

The distribution of the responses is presented in Table 20. The responses of the parents who originally took the child into their home as a foster child, and then later adopted, are not included in the table; these included 5 TRA couples and 1 IRA couple. (Foster placements are viewed as temporary, and foster parents are advised not to develop parental attachments to the child.)

Table 20

LENGTH OF TIME BEFORE PARENTS FELT CHILD WAS THEIR OWN

Length of Time Following Placement	TRA Parents N = 72		IRA Parents N = 80	
	Number	Percent	Number	Percent
Within a few days	37	51	61	76
1 Week	4	6	1	1
2 Weeks	3	4	5	6
3 Weeks	1	1	1	1
4 Weeks	6	8	2	3
6 Weeks	5	7	--	--
8 Weeks	2	3	2	3
3 Months	--	--	3	4
6 Months	2	3	2	3
7 Months	1	1	--	--
9 Months	1	1	--	--
1 Year	10	14	3	4
Totals	72	99	80	101

Most of the parents (51% of the TRA and 76% of the IRA) replied they felt the child was really their own within a few days after placement. Typical responses were "As soon as I held her," "Immediately," and "Upon seeing him."

Those parents indicating a length of time longer than 2 months were asked:

Why do you think it took this length of time?

There were 14 TRA parents and 8 IRA parents who specified a period of time longer than 2 months. Ten of these 22 parents explained several months passed before the child began to respond affectionately; 6 parents replied it takes awhile to develop a feeling of being a parent to a child; 3 parents mentioned they first fully had this feeling when the adoption was finalized and knew the child was legally their own; and 3 husbands indicated the lapse of time was due to limited contact with the child because of employment demands on their time.

The data in Table 20 shows a tendency for IRA parents to develop the parental feeling sooner than TRA parents. One explanation for this tendency is IRA parents, because they are more likely to be childless, perhaps more anxiously looked forward to being a parent and "worked harder" on trying to be a parent. Another explanation is related to the age of the children at the time of placement. The TRA children tended to be slightly older, which may have meant they were more apt to have developed stronger attachments to other adults in the past; only to have such attachments broken by separation. Because of such prior experience, they may have been more reserved in forming attachments to their adoptive parents; and the parents may not have felt the child was really their own until the child began to respond affectionately. A third explanation is that the physical features of a Black child may have contrasted more sharply from the parents' prior expectations of what a son or daughter of theirs would look like, and therfore may have slightly prolonged the development of parental feelings.

Reactions to Adoption

A) Reactions of Relatives: The TRA and IRA couples were asked during the interview two questions about the reactions of their relatives to the adoption:

a) What were the reactions of your relatives when the first heard you were going to adopt _____ (CHILD)?

b) How do these people feel about _____ (CHILD) now?

Only five of the 44 TRA couples reported no negative reactions from any relatives when informed of the adoption. Typical comments expressed by these couples were that relatives were "delighted," "excited," "pleased," "encouraging," and "proud of us." The other 39 TRA couples reported negative responses were received from some of their relatives. (Of these 39 couples, 26 also reported positive or neutral reactions from other relatives.) Generally the initial reaction appeared to be one of shock. For example, one mother mentioned upon informing her parents on the telephone about the impending adoption, her father was speechless and her mother began to cry. Following the initial shock, the negative reactions received ranged from minor misgivings to outspoken disapproval. Examples of mild negative responses were such questions as: if they thought they could love an adopted child as much as their natural born child; if they were financially able to care for another child; and if they had considered various problems which may arise as a result of adopting a child of another race. A majority of the 44 TRA families mentioned a few of their relatives expressed major opposition, with a number of these relatives attempting to discourage the couples from adopting. Some of the intense negative comments received as reported by the TRA couples were:

"You can't love someone not of your own blood"

"You have such a beautiful family, why do you want to spoil it"

39

"You're contributing to a social problem by making it easier for such people to have illegitimate children"

"They're better off with their own kind"

"If there is a race war, which side are you going to be on"

"Do you want _____ (natural born daughter) to marry a black man"

"Do you want people to think you're married to a black man."

In response to the second question regarding how the relatives now feel toward the child, it appears the opposition has subsided substantially; all of the parents mentioned the child has been fully accepted as part of the family by most (or all) of the relatives, even by many of the previously outspoken critics. Twenty-nine couples (71%) reported no negative reactions from any relatives; in addition, most of these parents mentioned such positive responses from relatives as "once they saw her, they loved her," "they adore him," "has become a family favorite," "couldn't love her more if she had been born to us," and "is their pride and joy." Of the 15 couples reporting current negative reactions from a few relatives, the degree of negativeness appeared to range from mild to quite intense. An example of a mild reaction is reported by a mother who said her parents seem to feel uneasy when they appear in public with the child as they go out of their way to explain to people that the child is adopted. Examples of continued intense negative opposition are: two couples mentioned a relative refuses to touch the child; one parent reported her parents stopped writing; and one TRA mother mentioned she has been disinherited by her parents.

The IRA parents, in response to the two questions about their relatives' reactions to the adoption, mentioned (as might be expected) fewer negative reactions when the relatives first heard about the adoption, and also at the time of the follow-up interview. Only ten of the 41 IRA families reported negative responses from some relatives when they first heard about the adoption; with these responses tending to be mild; e.g., wondering why they wanted an additional child when they already had children; mentioning a preference for genetic children over adopted; suggesting the couple should wait a few more months to see if they could have a natural born child; and wondering if they could love an adopted child as much as a natural child. In addition, one couple reported the father's parents had difficulty in accepting the fact that their son was infertile. At the time of the follow-up interview, almost all of the IRA parents reported their relatives were very accepting of their adopted child; only two couples reported a few relatives had not fully accepted the child. As might be expected, the relatives of IRA parents tended to react to the adoption of a child, while relatives of TRA parents generally reacted to the race of the adopted child.

Prior to this study, three other studies investigated reactions of relatives to the adoption of a Black child by white parents; with the results generally being consistent with this study. Edgar, in a survey of 18 couples who were members of the Open Door Society, found a majority of the couples received criticism and opposition from some relatives about the advisability of adoption, per se, and/or the adoption of a child of another race. The closer the geographical location of the critics to the adopting family, the more concerned the TRA parents appeared to be about the criticism. When the critics met the adopted child, they became more accepting in most cases. However, two couples reported former relationships with some relatives had been discontinued.

The Social Planning Council of Metropolitan Toronto (1966), in a study of 21 TRA families, found 14 (67%) couples experienced opposition from their parents to the adoption. The opposition ranged from minor reservations about the outcome to outspoken disapproval. In two cases the objections were reported as being directed against the adoption, rather than at the race of the child. Nine of these 14 couples whose parents initially expressed disapproval, reported their parents became more accepting of the child with the passage of time, primarily because the child "had sold himself." (p. 58)

Falk (1970), as previously mentioned, had three groups of white adoptive families in his study; one group of 59 couples who adopted a child of Black ancestry, another group of 90 couples who adopted a child of Indian ancestry, and the third group of 170 couples who adopted a child of their own race. The three groups were asked to check on a seven point scale "If your parents were living at the time you adopted your child (of another race or mixed race for transracial parents), how did they feel about the adoption?" (p. 20). A majority of the responses for all three groups were positive, with the highest average estimates being given by intraracial adoptive couples, the next highest by couples adopting an Indian child, and the lowest estimates by couples who adopted a Black child. Consistent with other studies, this result suggests relatives are more approving of intraracial adoptions than of transracial (particularly Black).

B)   Reactions of Friends and Neighbors: The following two interview questions were asked in reference to this topic:

a)   What were the reactions of your friends and neighbors when they first heard you were going to adopt _____ (CHILD)?

b)   How do these people feel about _____ (CHILD) now?

In contrast to the length of answers about the reactions of relatives, the answers to these questions were shorter, which suggests there may have been fewer reactions from friends and neighbors than from relatives; or that the parents may have been less concerned about the reactions of friends and neighbors.

Neither the TRA families nor the IRA families reported any intense opposition or criticism from their friends, either at the time when first informed about the adoption or at the time of the follow-up interview. A large majority of friends when informed about the adoption were reported to show such positive reactions as being "encouraging," "enthusiastic," and "happy for the parents." The reactions of a few friends when informed about the adoption, were described as one of "surprise" or "curiosity" or "no response." One TRA couple mentioned their friends were much more understanding about the adoption than were relatives. Another TRA couple noted a few of their friends expressed pleasure over the adoption, because, among other reasons, "it would allow their children to learn more about black people." Seven of the TRA couples and four of the IRA couples stated they were told by friends their adoption had influenced these friends to either adopt or think about adopting a child.

The reactions of neighbors tended to be somewhat less enthusiastic and supportive, but in general also accepting. None of the TRA couples reported any of their neighbors directly expressed intense disapproval of the adoption, as was noted among some of their relatives. (This difference may partially be due to social norms which allow relatives to more fully express their negative feelings in regard to family-connected affairs). Thirteen of the TRA couples reported some of their neighbors expressed disapproving comments upon being informed of the adoption; such as, "Why do you want to adopt another child," "I don't think it is right to adopt a child of another race," and "Aren't you worried about problems as he grows up." Some of these 13 TRA couples also reported they had heard indirectly, via the grapevine, that some of their neighbors had made critical comments, such as, "What a foolish thing to do,"

"Why don't they think of their other kids," and "I wonder how they feel when they pick up a black child." One of these 13 couples reported a feeling of being ignored by their neighbors, another indicated a few people in their congregation stopped talking to them. Several of these 13 couples mentioned neighbors who were initially dis-approving, have since become more accepting of the adopted child. Two couples, how-ever, reported that one of their neighbors will not touch the adopted child; and an-other couple mentioned a neighbor will not converse with them. One TRA father indicated neighbors tend to view him as being "eccentric," because his values and style of life differs considerably from theirs.

The most negative incident reported was one TRA couple mentioned their landlord asked them to move out of their apartment because he said the neighbors did not want Black children living in the community.

Although the reactions of friends and neighbors to the transracial adoptions as reported by the TRA couples tended in general to be accepting, several of the parents noted more critical comments perhaps are being made when they are not present. What-ever negative reactions there are, the intensity is at such a low degree that it has not surfaced to present any problems for the TRA couples (except for the family that was asked to vacate their apartment).

In reference to the reactions of neighbors, one TRA family who moved into an all-white rural community, reported the following remarks made by a neighbor. The TRA family had been living in the community for some time and the father mentioned to a visiting neighbor that no problems related to the race of the adopted child had been encountered by them in the community. The neighbor replied, "That's not surprising, we (the people in the community) are much more concerned about rock festivals, mari-juana and hippies, than having a Black child living here."

An interesting sidelight is that some TRA parents note some people (including some of their friends, neighbors, and relatives) appear to act "unnaturally" when they first meet the Black child. Some tend to "gush" and give over-attention to the child, while others appear aloof and uncertain how to relate to the child.

As far as the reactions of neighbors to the IRA adoptions, these parents generally reported all of their neighbors were accepting of the adopted child. Only two IRA families reported some of their neighbors appeared to have mixed feelings at the time of adoption; these centered around questions about their desire to adopt when they al-ready had natural-born children.

The generally favorable (at least accepting) reaction of friends and neighbors to the adoption of a Black child has also been found in other studies. The Social Planning Council of Metropolitan Toronto (1966) found in a study of 21 TRA families that three-fourths of these families reported their close friends either approved of their decision or appeared to accept it with no particular reaction. One family re-ported one of their friends was "really horrified" upon being informed of the adop-tion. The remaining families described their friends as being sympathetic, with some of them occasionally making a critical remark such as, "It's alright now, but what about when he is in his teens?" (p. 59). In regards to the reaction of neighbors, half of the parents said the reaction was completely favorable; an additional six families reported they had no reason to believe their neighbors questioned the idea; and the remaining families reported no notable opposition to the transracial adoption.

The 18 TRA families in Edgar's study reported no apparent opposition to the transracial adoption. Falk (1968) found the responses of relatives and friends as reported by the adoptive couples, were generally positive; as might be expected, relatives and friends were reported as being slightly less approving of transracial adoption than of intraracial adoption. When relatives, friends, and neighbors were ranked according to their degree of approval of transracial adoption (as reported by the adoptive couples), friends were ranked as being most approving, relatives were next, with neighbors being the least approving.

C) <u>Reactions of Strangers</u>: The TRA couples were asked:

What have been the reactions of strangers when they discovered _____
(CHILD) is a member of your family?

This question appeared to have been interpreted in three different ways: a) Reactions of strangers who are unaware the child is a member of the TRA family, b) Reactions of strangers who are aware the child is a member of the family, but do not know the child has been adopted, and c) Reactions of strangers after becoming aware child was adopted.

An indication of the first interpretation was a response by a TRA mother who indicated she had been asked by a stranger if she was babysitting for the child. Another TRA mother indicated she was standing next to her child at a zoo, and someone asked the child where her mother was. A TRA father said most strangers assume he's a foster child.

In reference to the second interpretation, several responses were noted. Two TRA mothers reported strangers had commented, "The child must look like your husband." Another TRA mother reported that when she and the child are alone in public, she has perceived stares suggesting she has been unfaithful to her husband. A TRA father reported that Black men sometimes "scowl" when he and the child are alone in public. One TRA mother alone with her child in public overheard the remark, "She must sleep with Blacks." A few TRA couples reported being asked by strangers if the child was adopted.

Upon being informed the child has been adopted, TRA couples reported the reaction of strangers varied; surprise, shock, no particular reaction, and "gushing" were noted. (The gushing reaction included such statements as, "What a wonderful thing for you to do," wanting to touch the child's hair, and giving over-attention to the child.)

One TRA family reported receiving a 30-page anonymous, critical letter which stated the adopted child "would be better off with his own kind," and also implied the TRA husband might be the father of the child. Another TRA couple received a Ku Klux Klan pamphlet in the mail which described the philosophy of the Klan and asserted in detail that the white race was superior.

The above summary of reactions of strnagers primarily enumerates negative reactions, and may thereby give a more unfavorable representation of the reactions than is warranted. When it is remembered there are 44 families in the study group, the occurrence of such negative incidents is rare. In fact, most of the TRA families reported no adverse reactions from strangers. By far, the usual reactions of strangers as reported by the TRA couples are curious stares, surprise, and puzzled expressions. In addition, eight of the 44 couples reported most strangers do not recognize their child is part-Black as the child has few Negroid features. As indicated earlier, varying degrees of Negroid characteristics in part-Black children may evoke somewhat different social meanings to persons. Unfortunately, no reliable method has been developed to ascertain the degree of Negroid appearance of part-Black people (Falk, 1968), and therefore differences in reactions of people due to varying degrees of Negroid characteristics of the TRA children in this study could not be examined.

A few families also cited positive incidents. One TRA family, for example, who lived in an all-white community reported a newspaper published a story about their transracial adoption, and the family was "deluged" by letters praising them, many of which were accompanied by anonymous gifts of money.

The writer is aware of only one other study which investigated reactions of strangers to transracial adoption. The Social Planning Council of Metropolitan Toronto (1966) asked a question similar to the one used in this study, and found that none of the TRA parents reported any unpleasant incidents with strangers.

D) <u>Reactions of Other Children in Family</u>: Forty-two of the 44 TRA families, and 23 of the 41 IRA families had other children (either genetic or adopted) in the home at the time of the adoption. The adoptive couples with other children were asked,

    a)   How did your other children react to _____ (CHILD) when they first saw him/her?

    b)   How do they feel about _____ (CHILD) now?

For the children who were old enough to understand, the parents generally indicated they had informed and prepared these children for the adoption. The children were in almost all cases reported as "excited" and "looking forward" to the adoption. One TRA couple reported their child cried and objected to the upcoming adoption because he did not want to have a baby in the family, and another TRA couple reported one of their school-age sons had questions about how he would cope with comments from his peers about have a Black for a brother.

Upon seeing the adopted child for the first time, the initial reactions of the other children were reported as favorable in all cases. Typical comments by parents of the reactions of their children were "thought he's cute," "admired him" and "made her feel right at home."

Following placement, normal sibling relationships developed according to the parents and the adoption record material. The record material also reported that some sibling rivalry usually developed in families where the adopted child was close in age to another child in the family. In three families (two TRA and one IRA), a sibling who previously had been an only child, were reported to have displayed intense sibling jealousy for several weeks.

At the time of the follow-up interview, the other children were reported to have fully accepted the adopted child as a member of the family.

E) <u>Reactions of Children in the Neighborhood</u>: Another question asked during the interview was:

How does _____ (CHILD) get along with other children in the neighborhood?

No difficulties in acceptance of the adopted child by other children were noted by either the IRA or TRA families. Typical responses of the adoptive couples were, "fine," "no problems," "very well," "good, they have the usual squabbles of children that age." One TRA couple responded, "Great--little children don't notice racial differences. You have to learn to hate--you're not born that way." Only one TRA couple noted the race of the child appeared to make a difference, as they indicated they had indirectly heard two or three mothers told their children not to play with ours.

The TRA couples were also asked if their child had been teased or called names by neighborhood children because of the color of his skin. Only 8 (18%) of the 44 families mentioned they were aware their child had been called a derogatory name; the names reported were "Nigger," "dirty Negro," "chocolate drop" and "slave." Two of the children were reported to have returned home in tears after being called such a name. In response to a question about how these 8 TRA couples dealt with such comments, 4 reported they attempted to comfort their child if he seemed hurt. One TRA father further added he told his son "Black is beautiful." Four TRA couples indicated their child did not appear upset, and one of these parents further commented that name-calling is part of childhood which all children must face and learn to cope with.

In response to other related interview questions, 10 of the 44 TRA couples reported their adopted child had attended (or was currently attending) either kindergarten or nursery school, and all ten couples indicated their child had not experienced any difficulties due to race in these schools.

Satisfactions With Adoptive Experience

The TRA and IRA families were asked the following four questions which were designed to obtain information on specific satisfactions with their adoptive experiences:

a) Being a parent brings certain satisfactions, what has been the one most satisfying thing to you in having _____ (CHILD) in your home as your child? (Both spouses were requested to respond to this question)

b) What else have you found satisfying about having _____ (CHILD) in your home?

c) What do you see as _____'s (CHILD) special strengths? His/her good points?

d) What has _____ (CHILD) added to your lives?

Since most of the respondents specified more than one satisfaction in answering the first question, the responses to this question have been categorized together in Table 21 with the responses to the other three questions. The first two questions were broad in scope, permitting the parents to respond with varied focuses; such as satisfactions with being a parent; family relationship satisfactions with having the child in the home; acceptance of the child by the extended family and broader community; and satisfactions with particular characteristics of the child. If the respondents focused on specifying particular characteristics of the child in answering the first two questions, the third question was somewhat redundant, but was asked in either case. The respondents either mentioned a few additional characteristics or indicated they had already answered the question.

The fourth question relating to what the adoption has added to their lives, usually elicited more abstract responses about the meaning of the adoptive experience to the spouses. In a few cases, some dissatisfactions were noted, (such as more work or less freedom) and these have been tabulated along with other expressed dissatisfactions in Table 23.

Table 21

SPECIFIC PARENTAL SATISFACTIONS IN THE ADOPTIVE EXPERIENCE

		Number of Couples Expressing This Satisfaction	
List of Satisfactions		TRA (N = 41)	IRA (N = 41)
A. With Being a Parent (Subtotal)		38	54
To watch and help a child grow and develop		12	19
Enjoyable to be a parent to child(ren)		5	14
Providing a home to a child in need		7	2
Personal fulfillment		3	5
Child is dependent upon and needs us		2	4
Setting a good example for a child		2	3
Taking care of a child (feeding, dressing, etc.)		3	1
Increases altruism		0	4
Feel younger		2	0
Increases appreciation of simple things in life		1	0
See things differently through child's eyes		1	0
Mother no longer has to work		0	1
Became better acquainted with neighbors		0	1
B. With Characteristics of Child (Subtotal)		100	96
Personality, temperment, disposition		41	40
Intelligent		24	20
Physically attractive		10	8
Interests, skills, sex-appropriate activity		8	10
Well-coordinated, athletic		7	3
Advanced physical development		3	4
Well-behaved, easy to reason with		2	4
Physical health		3	2
Willingly shares with other children		2	2
Neat, clean		0	2
Truthful		0	1
C. With Having Child in Family (Subtotal)		83	108
Brought increased happiness to family (joy to have around)		20	21
Enjoyable affectionate responses between child-parent		5	18

Table 21 (Concluded)

List of Satisfactions	Number of Couples Expressing This Satisfaction	
	TRA (N = 41)	IRA (N = 41)
Increased parents' interest and purpose in life	6	15
Rounded out family--made family complete	1	20
Good companion and playmate for other siblings	7	7
Brought variety and a new dimension to family	7	6
Having a girl (or another girl) in family	6	4
Companion for parents	5	4
Increased awareness and concern for people who are subjected to discrimination	7	0
Brought family closer together	1	6
Helped family members to realize no differences between races	6	0
Facilitated social and emotional development of other siblings	0	4
Having a boy (or another boy) in family	4	0
Helped improve race relations	4	0
Led to friendships with other couples who adopted	3	1
Fills void left by deceased child	1	1
Led to improvement of relations with grandparents	0	1
D. With Acceptance of the Child (Subtotal)	24	6
Child is loved and accepted by other members of family	14	6
Child is accepted by community	5	0
Child is accepted by relatives	3	0
Child is accepted by neighbors	1	0
Child is accepted by friends	1	0
E. Miscellaneous (Subtotal)	1	1
Enjoyed adoption process	1	1
Total satisfactions	246	265

The satisfactions are listed in Table 21 and have been grouped into five categories: Satisfactions with;

a) Being a parent

b) Child's characteristics

c)   Having child in family

d)   Acceptance of the child

e)   Miscellaneous

In those cases where both spouses specified the same response, only one tally was made. Likewise, if a parent repeated a satisfaction, only a tally of one was recorded.

The most frequently cited item by both groups is satisfactions with certain aspects of the child's "personality, temperment, disposition." Similarly, Jersild and Associates (1949) in an extensive study of the joys and problems of child rearing found satisfactions with personality characteristics of the child was the item cited by the largest percentage of parents (in that study the children were the parents' genetic children).

One of the most notable aspects of the table is that, on most items, approximately the same number of TRA and IRA couples express the item as a satisfaction, implying TRA and IRA couples are experiencing similar satisfactions from adopting a child. The total number of satisfactions expressed by the two groups is also similar. The TRA couples expressed a total of 246 satisfactions, with a mean of 6.0 items per couple, and the IRA couples expressed 265 satisfactions, with a mean of 6.5 items per couple.

There are some differences. The items for which there is a tally difference of 5 or more between the IRA and TRA couples were noted. Using this arbitrarily-selected guideline, the IRA couples more frequently mentioned the following items:

To watch and help a child grow and develop

Enjoyable to be a parent to child(ren)

Enjoyable affectionate responses between child-parent

Increased parents' interest and purpose in life

Rounded out family--made family complete

Brought family closer together.

The explanation for these differences may primarily be related to the fact that IRA couples were much more likely to be childless at the time of the adoption. Since the TRA couples generally had children in the family, they may have been experiencing these satisfactions before the addition of the adopted child, and therefore were less apt to express these satisfactions during the interview.

The items expressed by at least 5 or more TRA than IRA couples are:

Providing a home to a child in need

Increased awareness and concern for people who are subjected to discrimination

Helped family members to realize no differences between races

Child is loved and accepted by other members of family

Child is accepted by community.

The first three items appear directly related to the race of the child. The last two items may also be; prior to placement TRA families may have been more concerned than IRA families about the child being accepted by their other children, by themselves and by the broader community. Acceptance of the child following placement may have relieved their concerns, thereby being a satisfaction.

It perhaps should be noted that as the children grow older, the satisfactions experienced by the parents may change somewhat. For example, in a study of older adopted children (with a majority being teenagers) Kadushin (1966) found the most frequently expressed satisfactions were those related to achievements of the children. However, Jersild's (1949) extensive study of parental joys and problems in rearing children found "a high degree of consistency from one age level to the next in the relative frequency of mention of many categories of satisfaction" (p. 72). Jersild's study group included 544 families, with children ranging in age from infants to young adults.

Near the end of the interview, the TRA couples were asked the following additional question:

What do you think are the special satisfactions obtained by white adoptive parents of a _Black_ child?

The distribution of the responses are presented in Table 22.

Table 22

SPECIAL SATISFACTIONS OBTAINED BY WHITE PARENTS WHO ADOPT A BLACK CHILD - Pros

List of Satisfactions	Number TRA Families Expressing Item (N = 44)
Providing a home to a child who otherwise may not have a permanent family	15
Making a positive contribution to improving race relations	12
None--receive same satisfactions as if child were white	8
Is a way to live one's beliefs	6
Verifies belief there is no difference between Blacks and whites	5
Leads to increased insight into black culture	4
Increases awareness of racial problems	4
Black (mixed-race) children are physically attractive	3
Increases sensitivity to prejudice and its effects	2
Increases insight into own prejudices	2
Leads to less prejudice among our other children	1
Leads to development of friendly relationships with Blacks	1
Do not view child as a Black	1

The TRA couple who replied "Do not view child as a Black" explained they perceive the child as being a member of the white race. (The interviewer noted the child has blond hair, light-colored skin, and no apparent Negroid features.) The parents added that originally the child was placed as a foster child, and stated they would not have adopted him if he would have had prominent Negroid features.

Many of the TRA couples, either in response to the above question, or at some other time during the interview, indicated they became "color-blind" shortly after adopting; i.e., they stopped seeing the child as a Black, and instead came to perceive the child as an individual, an individual who is a member of their family.

Prior research comparing specific satisfactions between TRA and IRA families is limited. Falk (1970), as was consistent with the results of this study, found TRA families were somewhat more apt to cite satisfactions in the area of human relationships (such as in seeing the racial attitudes of other people become more positive); while IRA families expressed more satisfactions in the area of parent-child relationships. Falk notes the latter finding was probably due to the IRA families having their first parental experiences.

Edgar, in a study of 18 TRA families, found the following responses to the question, "What special satisfactions, if any, are gained from interracial adoption?" Five families indicated no special satisfactions; seven indicated providing a home to a child in need; seven mentioned making a contribution towards interracial understanding; and seven specified broadening their circle of friends, including people of other races.

Dissatisfactions With Adoptive Experience

Table 23 presents the distribution of the dissatisfactions expressed by the adoptive parents in response to the following three interview questions:

a) As every parent knows, being a parent not only has satisfactions, but also some dissatisfactions. What has been the one most dissatisfying thing to you in having _____ (CHILD) in your home as your child? (Both spouses were requested to respond to this question)

b) What else have you found dissatisfying about having _____ (CHILD) in your home?

c) As any parent knows, all children have some faults, some shortcomings. What are _____'s (CHILD) shortcomings?

Some respondents also expressed some dissatisfactions in response to the question "What has _____ (CHILD) added to your lives?" These dissatisfactions were also tabulated and included in Table 23.

The dissatisfactions have been grouped in Table 23 into five categories. Dissatisfactions with,

a) Being a parent

b) Child's characteristics

c) Having child in family

d) Acceptance of the child

e) Miscellaneous.

If both spouses expressed the same dissatisfaction, or if one spouse repeated a dissatisfaction, only one tally was made.

Table 23

SPECIFIC PARENTAL DISSATISFACTIONS IN THE ADOPTIVE EXPERIENCE

List of Dissatisfactions	Number of Couples Expressing This Dissatisfaction	
	TRA (N = 41)	IRA (N = 41)
A. **With Being a Parent** (Subtotal)	23	20
Curtailment of previous activities ("more tied down")	12	11
Increased financial responsibility	5	5
Changing and washing diapers	5	2
Insufficient time to spend with family	0	1
Sharing spouse with children	1	0
Dislike disciplining child	0	1
B. **With Characteristics of Child** (Subtotal)	56	64
Personality, temperment, disposition	31	35
Disobedient, difficult to reason with	8	12
Routines (eating, sleeping, elimination)	8	9
Physical health	3	7
Physical size, strength, reactions	2	1
Thumbsucking, fingernail biting	3	0
Child displays few affectional responses to one parent	1	0
C. **With Child in Home** (Subtotal)	16	14
Increased confusions, frustrations, annoyanges	6	5
Sometimes interrupts parents' sleep	4	5
Relationship with siblings (fighting, teasing)	4	3
Home is more crowded	1	0
Inferences by some people one spouse has been unfaithful	1	0
Wears down parent	0	1
D. **With Acceptance of the Child** (Subtotal)	11	6
Reactions of relatives to adoption	2	2
Gushing reaction (e.g., "what a wonderful thing for you to do to adopt this child")	3	1
People react differently to adopted child than to genetic child (over-attention or less attention)	3	1
People stare at when in public with adopted child	2	0

51

Table 23 (Concluded)

List of Dissatisfactions	Number of Couples Expressing This Dissatisfaction	
	TRA (N = 41)	IRA (N = 41)
Sibling rivalry when child first arrived	0	2
Hesitant to take adopted child into black community for fear of disapproval	1	0
E. Miscellaneous (Subtotal)	0	1
Accepting infertility status	0	1
Total Dissatisfactions	106	105

An examination of Table 23 shows the most frequently expressed dissatisfactions were about the child's "Personality, temperment, disposition." In relation to this item 25 couples expressed dissatisfaction with the child's "temper," and 21 about the child's "being stubborn." Similarly, Jersild (1949) found dissatisfactions with the child's personality characteristics was the item cited by the largest percentage of parents.

On almost all items, approximately the same number of TRA and IRA families express the item as a dissatisfaction. The total number of dissatisfactions expressed by the two groups is also similar. The TRA group expressed a total of 106 dissatisfactions, with a mean of 2.6 items per couple; and the IRA group expressed 105 dissatisfactions, with a mean of 2.6 items per couple.

Only a few of the dissatisfactions expressed by the TRA families appeared to be related to the race of the child, such as,

People react differently to adopted child than to genetic child (over-attention or less attention)

People stare at when in public with adopted child

Inferences by some people one spouse has been unfaithful

Hesitant to take adopted child into black community for fear of disapproval

Gushing reaction (e.g., "what a wonderful thing for you to do to adopt this child").

The number of TRA couples indicating these items as dissatisfactions were very few; of the five items, there were only a total of 10 tallies (an average of 2 per item).

TRA couples, it perhaps should be pointed out, were not alone in receiving the "gushing reaction" to the adoption. Several of the IRA couples also indicated at other points during the interview they had heard such remarks as "how wonderful it is for you to provide this child with a home" and "what a charitable thing to do." Both TRA and IRA couples mentioned they find such comments irritating as they do not view their adoption as a "saintly" act; rather they feel they adopted because of anticipated personal gratifications they would receive from having a child (or another child) in their family. A typical related comment mentioned by some of these couples was "we feel we are receiving more from the child than we are giving."

A comparison of interest is the ratio of satisfactions to dissatisfactions for the two groups. Table 21 presents the parental satisfactions, showing TRA couples expressed a total of 246 satisfactions, while the IRA couples expressed a total of 265 satisfactions. Table 23 presents the parental dissatisfactions, with TRA couples expressing a total of 106 dissatisfactions, and IRA couples expressing 105 dissatis- factions. The satisfaction-dissatisfaction ratio for both groups is approximately 2.5:1. Interestingly, Jersild (1949) obtained a similar ratio of satisfactions to dissatisfactions, even though he used somewhat different categories and procedures (p. 21).

The special problems TRA families may encounter because of the race of the adopted child was explored further by asking later in the interview:

What special problems do you think white adoptive parents of a Black child face?

The distribution of the responses is presented in Table 24.

Table 24

SPECIAL PROBLEMS TRA COUPLES BELIEVE WHITE ADOPTIVE PARENTS OF A BLACK CHILD ENCOUNTER

Problems	Number of TRA Couples Expressing Problem (N = 41)
Helping child to understand black culture and establish an identity	12
Helping child (when older) to understand why he may be subjected to discrimination	8
Criticism from relatives, neighbors, and friends	5
Reactions of white people in community who disapprove	5
Unaware of any	4
Disapproval of the adoption by some Blacks	3
Impact of Black child on other children in family	2
Development of special problems will depend on where family lives	2
Inferences of unfaithfulness to spouse	1
Handling own prejudices and stereotypes	1
Perhaps some difficulty (by the TRA parents) in obtaining employment	1
Receiving stares from other peopld	1
Reaction of black child to being raised in a white family	1
Anticipating more problems than will arise	1

One of the most notable features of Table 24 is very few special problems are expressed by these families; the 44 couples mentioned a total of 43 items--just under one item per family. The small number suggests TRA couples, after having an adopted Black child in their home for a couple of years, believe transracial adoption presents few special problems.

53

Most of the special problems mentioned can be classified into two broad categories; a) Difficulties the adopted Black child will encounter in establishing an identity and coping with discrimination. b) Negative responses received by parents from other people due to the adoption.

Anticipation of Future Problems

In separate questions, the TRA couples were asked if they expect their child will have any particular problems due to race in elementary school, in seeking employment, and in dating. The distribution of the replies is presented in Table 25.

Table 25

TRA COUPLES' EXPECTATIONS OF FUTURE PROBLEMS
FOR THEIR CHILD DUE TO RACE

Problem Area	Problem Anticipated (N = 44)	No Problem Anticipated (N = 44)	Do Not Know (N = 44)
Elementary School	11	28	5
Employment	16	20	8
Dating	37	5	2

A majority (28 of the 44 couples--64%) mentioned they do not anticipate their child will have any special problems due to race in elementary school. Reasons given for anticipating no problems were: the child already knows and has a good relationship with many of the children he will be attending school; the school which the child will be attending is integrated and apparently has no race problems; the child has a "likable" personality; and the child has few Negroid features and probably will not be viewed as being a Black.

The 11 couples who anticipate some problems may arise, generally indicated they expect such problems will be minor in nature, with name-calling being the most frequently cited difficulty (some of these respondents minimized this problem by indicating all children are subjected to name-calling by peers). Other problems noted were that prejudiced teachers may subtly discriminate, some parents may not want their children to play with a Black child, and the child may be less likely to be invited to parties.

Sixteen families indicated their child (when older) may have some difficulty due to race in obtaining employment. One of these families also commented fellow workers may not be as friendly because of their son's race. Most of the 20 families who stated they did not expect problems in this area mentioned they anticipate race relations would be improved by the time their child is of employment age. Several families pointed out substantial progress is presently being made in breaking down barriers to employment because of race. Five of the TRA families noted if their child receives a college education, there should be no trouble in obtaining employment. Most of the 8 families who mentioned they are uncertain if their child will have problems due to race in obtaining employment, noted the development of such problems would depend on the type of employment sought, the community where one is located, and the nature of race relations at that time.

Although few (and relatively minor) problems were anticipated in elementary school and in seeking employment, TRA families generally expected more serious problems due to race will develop for their child in the dating area. Thirty-seven (84%) couples anticipated problems will occur due to race, with 24 of these couples noting they believe problems will primarily arise from objections by parents of the potential dates. Four of the TRA couples mentioned other white parents are apt to have fewer objections to a white son of theirs dating a black person, than a daughter, because of more concern about a daughter becoming sexually involved (particularly with someone of a different race). Three TRA couples commented their daughter may be subjected to considerable pressure from white dates to have pre-marital relations. Two TRA couples speculated Black parents of a potential date may object because the adopted child has white parents. Three couples anticipate their adopted son may experience some rejection due to race when asking girls for dates. Six couples stated their child will, before beginning to date, face an identity decision over whether to date Blacks or whites.

The five couples anticipating no dating difficulties due to race gave as reasons: have seen interracial dating work out; barriers to interracial dating are breaking down; many potential dates will have known the TRA person since childhood and will view him as a person rather than as a Black; and child has a "lovable" personality. Of the two couples who indicated uncertainty about problems arising, one stated "it will depend on where we live," and the other replied, "we'll find out, then, who are real friends are."

In comparing these results to other studies, Edgar found, consistent with this study, that a higher percentage of TRA families anticipated problems in the area of dating, than in attending elementary school or in seeking employment. Similar problems were expected as mentioned in this study.

Falk (1970) found 35% of the transracial parents anticipate their child might experience difficulties in school due to race, such as teasing and heckling. Falk (1970) further reports 42% of the 52 transracial adoptive parents whose children were attending school reported difficulties due to race.

In the area of dating, Falk reports 35% of the transracial parents anticipated difficulties due to race, such as objections by parents of dates and rejection by potential dates. This percentage (35%) is considerably lower than the 84% found in this study. The reason for this inconsistency is unclear. It may partially be related to the race of the child; more than half of the transracial couples in Falk's study adopted a child of Indian ancestry, and such parents may anticipate fewer dating difficulties than parents who adopt a Black child. Unfortunately, Falk does not provide a breakdown of responses for the two types of transracial adoptive placements.

An area of interest not examined in this study is TRA couples' attitudes toward cross-racial dating and marriage. Falk (1968), however included items on this subject in his questionnaire and found transracial adoptive parents generally approve of both cross-racial dating and marriage, while intraracial adoptive parents are generally opposed to both.

Establishing an Identity

The difficulties a black child reared in a white home may experience in developing an identity is currently a major concern (Falk, 1968; Open Door Society, 1970). In an effort to explore this area, the TRA couples were asked:

What special problems do you think a Black child adopted by White parents will have in establishing a self-identity?

Eighteen of the families expressed concern that their child may have problems in this area. These couples speculated their child as he grows older may have difficulty in deciding, "Where do I belong," "Who am I," "Am I white--am I black, where do I fit in." Two of these 18 couples noted their child may also have difficulty in understanding why he is subjected to discrimination.

Sixteen of the couples mentioned they do not expect their child will experience any special problems in this area; most indicated they felt by giving the child guidance and love during his formative years, he would establish a healthy self-identity. Some added they intend to expose the child to black culture in order to instill a sense of pride in both the black and white races. The parents' motives for instilling a sense of pride in both races are not entirely clear. Some parents may feel that exposure to black culture will help the child to understand why in future years he may be subjected to discrimination. Other couples may feel that if their child is in future years faced with having to decide which race to identify with, exposure to black culture will help prepare the TRA person to make the decision, and to then live with that decision.

Ten couples mentioned they are uncertain if their child will have problems in establishing a self-identity, with a number of these parents indicating by their comments they had concerns in this area.

In assessing the significance of the identity problem, there unfortunately has been no decisive research (at least that the writer is aware of) conducted on the dynamics which are likely to occur. Since the placement of Black children for adoption in white homes is of recent origin, it may not be possible for a few more years to gather research data on identity formation problems which may develop during adolescence and in adulthood. There are, however, other comparative types of child care arrangements that have been of longer duration and could currently be investigated; such as Black children reared in white foster homes, mulatto children raised by one parent who is black and the other white, and Oriental and Indian children who have been adopted by white parents. The latter types of transracial placements have been in existence for over two decades. It is rather surprising, with the current concern over identity in transracial placements, that research has apparently not been conducted on any of these types of arrangements.

Falk (1968) points out various outcomes of identity formation can be developed by using different theoretical concepts. Two of these will be presented here, one which suggests the processes involved in forming identity for TRA parents may lead to serious problems, while the other deduces a much more favorable outcome.

The first formulation is one of several developed by Falk (1968). Several writers have noted there are special meanings and values associated with being a Black (see e.g., Grossack, 1965; Bernard, 1966; and Fishman, 1967). A Black child learns these special meanings and values through being raised by his natural parents and by living in a Black community. Furthermore, numerous white people react to Blacks in terms of stereotypes (rather than as person), which the Black child learns to cope with. However, a Black child reared in a white family learns the values of his white middle class parents, and also may be less exposed during his childhood years to stereotyping by white people. Falk goes on to state,

> ... at some point the TRA child will cast off the protectiveness of the family of orientation and establish his more-or-less independent identity in the community of his choosing. If in this new circumstance he finds himself forced into situations where he is identified stereotypically and he is without prior experience in coping with them, he may face an identity crisis .... His identity will be with the white world while others assume that his identity is with the black world. His rearing establishes the white world as his referent, and his new peers demand that his referent be the minority world. (p. 64)

Furthermore, if unable to identify with white people in a new community, he may attempt to identify with black people. However, because his values and experiences have been quite different, he may only be permitted limited membership in his new social group and become a marginal person (Thompson, 1966).

The second formulation is a composite of certain aspects of identity formation taken from Erikson (1963), Falk (1968), and Hagen (1970). Identity is one's perception of self; the way a person perceives himself in relation to the world in which he lives. Hagen (1970) notes, "a positive identity is when a person feels good about the image one has of himself and feels that the characteristics of himself are accepted and approved by others" (p. 10). Formation of an individual's identity is a gradual, continual process. If a child is given the necessary guidance and affection by his parents, according to social-psychological theory, he will begin to develop a positive self-concept and social skills for effectively dealing with his environment. During childhood, a Black child reared in a white home will also be exposed to some white people who react to him in terms of stereotypes about his race, rather than in terms of him as an individual; however, with the emotional support and explanations of his parents he ought to begin developing techniques of dealing with stereotype reactions. Exposure to black history and culture, and also perhaps contact with other Blacks, should further provide him with a fuller comprehension of the meanings and values associated with the Black race.

With such a preparation, it may well be that a Black child reared by white parents may be as capable of dealing with stereotype reactions to his race as other Black children reared by their natural parents. In addition, a TRA person, when older, may have an added advantage of being better prepared to form positive relationships with white people, due to his childhood experiences in which he formed close relations with his white parents and siblings, and also was exposed and perhaps acquired many of the values of his white parents. Furthermore, since TRA parents generally have a high socio-economic status, they are apt to encourage and assist their adopted child in obtaining a high education, which should further develop the TRA person's capacity to financially and personally find a place in society. It may be that a TRA person, instead of becoming a marginal person, will be as well-equipped (or even better prepared) to form a positive identity than a Black child reared in a Black home.

These are only two suggested alternatives to identity formation, and probably represent the polar extremes. Numerous other alternatives could also be developed. The writer's personal opinion, for whatever it is worth, is that the speculated problems related to identity formation for the TRA person have been over-exaggerated.

In relation to the identity question, the writer wishes to speculate there may be an additional advantage for a Black child to be raised by white parents that has, as far as the writer is aware, been overlooked. Various writers (e.g., Griffin, 1961) have noted many Blacks feel inferior to whites. This inferior feeling is part of one's identity, and is likely to be conveyed to their children and become part of their children's self-concept; i.e., their identity (Erikson, 1963). White adoptive parents are unlikely to have feelings of racial inferiority, and may thereby convey this more positive aspect of identity to their Black children.

In regards to the question of whether a TRA person will identify with the white race or with the black race, this writer wonders how important an identification in this area will loom to the TRA person. Identifying with a race is certainly not the only identification as TRA person can make. There are many other groups that a person has an opportunity to identify with, such as peers, family, friends, church and school groups, professional and trade groups, recreational and social groups, etc.

Furthermore, the writer believes the question of which race a TRA person will identify with is not the real question at issue. To identify means to take on the characteristics and goals of others as one's own (Hagen, 1970). It is difficult to determine the characteristics of either the white or black race, since there is so much variation within subgroups of these races. For example, it is likely that upper class Blacks have more characteristics in common with upper class whites than with lower class Blacks. However, characteristics of subgroups of races probably can be identified. For example, NAACP members probably have some common goals, values, and methods of proceeding. Therefore, the question of which race a TRA person will identify with probably needs rephrasing to: Will TRA persons identify with subgroups of either the black or white race? If the answer is affirmative, an interesting question is which subgroups they are likely to identify with.

Reflections About Adoptive Experience

Both TRA and IRA couples were asked:

Looking back on your experience with _____ (CHILD), in what ways, if any, is it different from what you anticipated, expected, or pictured it to be?

The distribution of the responses is presented in Table 26.

Most of the IRA parents interpreted the question in terms of ways in which agency adoption procedures differed from their expectations prior to applying. Since such responses did not appear to have any implications for transracial adoptions or suggest changes in agency adoption procedures, these replies have been grouped together in Table 26 under the heading "Certain aspects of agency adoption procedures were different than anticipated."

Of greater interest are the responses of the TRA parents who interpreted the question in terms of the desired set; i.e., ways in which their adoptive experiences differed from their expectations prior to adopting. Twenty-five (61%) couples mentioned they had either received fewer negative reactions (or none at all) from other people than they had anticipated. Apparently these families had anticipated a fair amount of criticism, and perhaps other forms of negative response, to the adoption because of the race of the child. Two other replies of TRA couples are consistent with this interpretation: "Child is better accepted by grandparents than anticipated,"

Table 26

WAYS IN WHICH ADOPTION EXPERIENCES WERE DIFFERENT THAN ANTICIPATED

Specific Differences Mentioned	TRA Families (N = 41)	IRA Families (N = 41)
Certain aspects of agency adoption procedures were different than anticipated	--	29
Fewer (or no) negative reactions from other people	25	--
No differences	7	5
Child was more easily accepted as member of family	9	2
Child is lighter in color than expected	3	--
Child is easier to care for	1	2
We (parents) are less self-conscious of child's color	2	--
Child is better accepted by grandparents than anticipated	2	--
Child is more wonderful than imagined	1	1
No sibling jealousy developed	--	2
Soon forgot child is adopted	--	1
Other people did not as readily accept child	1	--
Child is better accepted by other people	1	--
Expected more people to stare	1	--
Stares of people at times make me feel like I'm black	1	--
Friends were delighted by adoption	1	--
Fewer behavioral problems manifested by child	1	--
Took a long time for child to adjust to family	--	1
Total Differences Cited	49	38

and "Child is better accepted by other people." Such comments are an indication the parents have encountered fewer problems related to the race of the child than anticipated. Agency record material also support this conclusion. After placement, agencies maintain contact with the adoption family until finalization of the adoption (which usually takes place about a year after placement). Very few incidents related to race are recorded in the record material, with the records in all cases indicating the agency is satisfied with the outcome at the time of finalization. Typical summary comments in the records are:

"The _____'s (parents) have experienced no unusual incidents directly relating to the fact they have adopted an interracial child. Relatives and friends have wholeheartedly accepted _____ (CHILD) into the family and the _____'s (parents) are extremely proud of their daughter."

"The adoptive parents have not encountered many of the problems commonly thought of as possible occurrences in an interracial adoption."

59

Interest in Open Door Society

The Wisconsin Division of Family Services requested at the time when the interview schedules were being developed, that the TRA adoptive couples' interest in joining the Open Door Society be surveyed. The Open Door Society is an organization composed of transracial adoptive couples, with local chapters in the United States and Canada. Its stated aims are,

To encourage the general acceptance, throughout the community, of children throughout the community, of children of minority races or mixed background, to promote the legal adoption of such children by parents of any race, and in this connection to work as closely as possible with official adoption agencies. (McCrea, 1967)

The organization also provides an opportunity for transracial adoptive parents to share and discuss their experiences and concerns.

The TRA couples were asked two questions in reference to the Open Door Society:

a. Would you be interested in periodically getting together with other couples who have adopted a child of another race in order to share and discuss your experiences and concerns?

The responses of the 44 TRA couples were:

28 Yes   13 No   3 Uncertain

b. Are you presenting a member, or have you thought about joining the Open Door Society?

The responses of the 44 TRA couples were:

8   Member

2   Nonmember, interested in joining

17 Nonmember, not interested in joining

6   Have not heard of Open Door Society

11 Am member of some other similar organization

Two other groups similar to the Open Door Society have been formed in Wisconsin; the Inter-Racial Family group in Madison, and an informal group of transracial adoptive families in Brown County.

Suggested Changes in Adoption Procedures

Near the end of the interview the adoptive parents were asked:

One of the reasons for doing this study is to obtain suggestions for ways in which adoptive agencies can improve their services to couples who are in the process of adopting a child. What do you think your agency might have done differently to help make your experience as adoptive parents more successful and satisfying?

Most of the IRA and TRA parents mentioned they were very pleased with the services received from the agency through which they adopted a child, and 13 couples

60

indicated they had no suggestions for changes. Seventy-two couples (85%) indicated they questioned certain aspects of the adoption process, with a number of these families suggesting changes.

Before presenting the responses to this question, it should be pointed out the purpose of this thesis is not to evaluate agency procedures, and the author does not contend to possess expertise in this area. Rather, the author believes recipients of services, by having gone through the procedures, are in a unique position to identify aspects of the process that have not been beneficial to either the child or themselves, and may formulate worthy suggestions for changing those aspects. Most of the adoptive parents in this study have a high education, and therefore are apt to be quite perceptive in identifying weaknesses in agency procedures.

The intention of the writer in presenting these suggested changes is not to urge the changes be made, but simply to inform agencies of these comments and suggestions. Agency staff have more direct experience with adoption procedures than the author, and therefore may be more qualified to determine if the suggestions have merit.

In addition, it should be noted agencies have made a number of changes in the last few years since the time when the parents in this study were involved in the adoption process; therefore it is possible some of the suggestions have already been (or are presently being) incorporated into agency programs.

1. Increased staff commitment to transracial adoption: Six TRA couples reported their adoption worker appeared to question the desirability of transracial adoption, and seemed reluctant to place a Black child with them. In connection with this suggestion, Mitchell (1969) notes:

For success in an agency program of transracial placements, the administration and the professional staff must be convinced that there are families that can accept the challenge with regard to the extended family and the community, and still be able to provide warmth and security for the child. (p. 614)

It is hoped this study and similar research will aid adoption workers in arriving at a decision regarding the merits of transracial adoption.

2. Increased promotion of transracial adoption: Four TRA families urged increased publicity via television, radio, and press to promote transracial adoptions. Mitchell (1969) indicates such publicity programs have been quite successful in locating white adoptive parents for Black children. One of the more innovative and apparently successful techniques has been to show pictures of children needing homes via the news media. In addition, one TRA couple recommended increased development of adoption resource exchanges covering larger geographical areas.

3. Agencies should better inform prospective transracial adoptive applicants about the experiences they are likely to encounter: Six TRA couples made this suggestion. This suggestion probably should not be interpreted as a criticism of agencies, as TRA placements have been of such recent origin that there has been very limited feedback on the experiences that have been encountered. Again, it is hoped that such research as this study will be useful in providing information to both adoption workers and adoptive applicants. In connection with this topic, three TRA parents

suggested it would be helpful for prospective transracial adoptive applicants to talk to parents who have adopted a Black child.

4. Agencies should subsidize adoptions by low income families: This suggestion was made by one TRA family and five IRA families. Coverage of medical expenses was thought of particular importance by four of these families. Three families mentioned agencies should give more consideration to the attitudes of applicants rather than the financial resources. A few private agencies in the state have already subsidized adoptions for special cases, and the State Division of Family Services is giving careful consideration to this idea. Other states, such as New York have initiated such programs.

In connection with this suggestion, Hagen (1969) notes;

We realize the validity of subsidized adoption, but are held back because of the traditional attitudes that adoption is for those who can't have their own. Thus we hear statements such as "if they want a child they should be willing to pay for his care," or "what is their motivation if they want money for caring for a child." Potential parents may be uncomfortable about receiving a subsidy for similar reasons.

In order for subsidized adoption to be valid, there must be a more clear and defined concept that adoption is not only a way for a childless couple to get a child, but is also directed to making it possible for children to have homes. A child is not dependent on who is willing to accept him, but society is interested in him. There are people who can be parents; other people can help provide for his needs for food, clothing and medical care.

It seems we should direct our program to the people who can best care for these children. The couples who have adopted children with physical handicaps, older children, or of another race than themselves are usually couples who have children. They don't need a child in the same way as does a childless couple. Their motive is more to provide a home for a child. Because they already have children these couples can least afford additional responsibility.

It does not seem appropriate to require potential parents to pay for a child's expenses when they respond to our request for homes. (p. 16)

5. Adoption practice should be based on an enabling approach rather than a diagnostic approach: A number of both TRA and IRA parents were critical of certain aspects of the diagnostic approach whish is used by most adoptive workers. A description of the diagnostic approach is provided by Hagen (1969):

Much of present practice has been influenced by the diagnostic school of thought. According to this theory, a person is influenced, or determined, by his past experiences. In order to know a person, one must know his life experiences and the meaning this had for him. If his experiences are essentially positive, the person is probably emotionally healthy. If experiences have been negative, a person must gain insight, or work through his conflict or, have his emotional needs met in other ways. Practice under the diagnostic approach is thus based on getting information about significant areas of development and current functioning in order to decide if a particular coupld should be approved or not. It is a natural choice according to the theories on which much of social work has been based. (p. 2)

In reference to this approach, two couples indicated they had the feeling they were on trial and could not relax during the interviews. Three couples questioned whether the lengthy home study could not have been shortened. Three couples mentioned many of the questions asked by the adoption workers seemed meaningless; one of these parents emphasized this point by stating the caseworker "asked too many insignificant dull, dreary, boring questions." Another family complained that when they asked questions related to being an adoptive parent, the worker would not provide an opinion or information, but rather return the question by asking what the applicants thought in regards to the question. One family mentioned the pre-adoptive interviews went into too much detail about their backgrounds, with the parents noting they were able to detect the psychological implications of the questions and therefore generally attempted to provide an answer that the agency would find acceptable. Three couples mentioned agencies approach adoptive applicants "suspiciously," with two of these couples specifically recommending agencies should rather employ the "enabling" approach recently developed by Clayton Hagen, adoption supervisor at Lutheran Social Services of Minnesota.

This approach is goal or future oriented; it is based on the assumption that a person is motivated more by his goals than by his past. Even if a person has had negative experiences in the past, this approach assumes such early experiences do not have to be resolved before the person can move on to new experiences. More importantly, a person needs to consider his present abilities and goals, and then choose the courses of action which will enable him to achieve his goals.

Issac (1965) summarizes the ways in which adoption practice based on the enabling approach differs from the diagnostic approach;

The whole function of the social worker shifts from that of judge to that of colleague and helper, as she comes to see herself as a person who helps applicants to become more confident and secure adoptive parents.

In the view of Lutheran Social Services of Minnesota the present approach has made agencies of far less help to adoptive families than they could or should be. For if would-be parents feel they are going to be judged as fit or unfit parents, their whole effort is bent upon trying to mold themselves into their idea of what the agency looks for in an adoptive couple. If there is anything that they feel might make them appear less desirable in the agency's eyes, they seek to hide it. If they have questions and doubts about adoption, they certainly seek to hide them, for there is always the danger the agency will decide they are ambivalent or unready for parenthood. The couple consider themselves on trial and, as anyone who is on trial, seek to present a convincing picture of their own right conduct and suppress any evidence that might throw question on it. But, according to Hagen, an agency can only really come to know and help adoptive applicants if they are encouraged to be frank and say what they really thing without fear that anything they say may be held against them. Instead of challenging applicants to answer the agency's questions, the agency encourages the applicants to ask the agency their own questions, voice their own concerns, make their own demands. The agency of course reserves the right not to place a child with applicants, but if something comes up that makes the social worker feel the agency cannot place a child with the couple, the couple is immediately told of this. If the problem can be ironed out it will be, and if not the couple will drop out. There is no series of interviews at the end of which a couple must anticipate a favorable or unfavorable judgment--with little notion of what it will be until it comes and even then of why it is what it is. The whole adoptive study is focused on trying to help adoptive applicants feel like parents and to give them an understanding of what the special problems and rewards of adoption are likely to be; applicants are not made to feel like candidates for a modeling job whose measurements may or may not turn out to be right.

6. <u>Length of time between placement and finalization of adoption should be shortened</u>: Two families made this suggestion, indicating the currently used policy of approximately one year unnecessarily keeps families in suspense for too long; knowing there is a chance the child may be removed.

7. <u>Adoption fees between agencies should be standardized</u>: One family made this suggestion.

8. <u>The requirement that the religion of the natural mother be the same as that of the adoptive parents should be discontinued</u>: One family made this suggestion as they felt the requirement leads to delays in placing children into adoptive homes. The stated philosophy of the Child Welfare League of America (Standards for Adoption, 1968) is that religious matching should be practiced where practicable, but not where it means placement would be delayed or result in the child being placed in a less suitable home. In most states, however, state statutes or administrative regulations, ensure that religious lines will not be crossed, and there is evidence that such a requirement leads to delays in placement. (Issac, 1965)

9. <u>Agencies should offer to provide the services of an attorney</u>: This suggestion was made by one family. Another family commented they felt the attorney's fee was too high, and another family wondered whether the services of an attorney were even needed.

10. <u>Agencies should provide parents with a children's book that would be designed to help the child understand he is adopted</u>: This suggestion was made by one IRA family.

CHAPTER V

OVERALL OUTCOME OF TRANSRACIAL ADOPTIONS

Review of Prior Outcome Studies

A.   Intraracial Adoptions: Kadushin (1967) made an extensive review of adoption outcome studies, and prepared a summary table of the findings. With the author's kind permission, this table has been reproduced and included as Table 27 in this thesis. Kadushin notes summaries of follow-up studies on groups of children with special problems (racially mixed children, older children, and foreign-born children placed for adoption in the United States) are not included in this table. Furthermore, the summarization only includes those studies in which the sources of data, outcome criteria, and outcomes were explicitly stated.

Inspection of Table 27 reveals considerable variation among studies in many crucial ways; in terms of the outcome criteria employed, in the types of data used for follow-up assessment, in the size of study group, and in the length of time between placement and outcome assessment.

Added together, there are a total of 1824 adopted children in these studies. If the findings for these studies are combined, the average "success" rate varies between 74% to 86%, depending on how many of the intermediate success categories are included in the success group. This success rate provides a useful comparison to the outcome rate for the transracial adoptions to be presented later in this chapter.

Since Kadushin's review, an additional outcome study by Kornitzer (1968) has been published. The study was conducted over a period of 13 years, and involved interviews with 503 adoptive couples. The study design was not very rigorous. The primary outcome criterion employed was the interviewer's judgment of the overall success. Although the ages of the children at time of follow-up are not provided, the author notes all of the children for which outcomes were rated were older than four years of age. Outcome judgments of the success of the placements are only reported for selected groups of children--a total of 233 children. The distribution of the interviewer's ratings of the outcome of these placements were: 41.2% "success"; 36.5% "average"; 19.3% "problems"; and 3.0% "bad or failed." (p. 159)

B.   Transracial Adoptions: Few studies have examined the outcome of interracial adoptions. In one, Graham (1957) assessed the outcome of 50 Japanese children adopted by Americans (many of these Americans had been associated with civilian or military agencies in Japan). The study data were obtained from interviews with the adoptive couples, and the children's teachers. Among the factors considered in the outcome were quality of relationship with adoptive parents and siblings, symptoms of maladjustment attributable to post-placement development, and comfort in awareness of original identity. The outcome rating was based on the judgment of the interviewer, with 64% of the children were rated as having "satisfactory adoptive adjustment and very good prognosis"; 26% were rated as "only fair" and 10% were considered "poor" or "very poor." Cultural adjustments were not regarded as a significant factor in adjustment.

Valk (1957) reports on the initial adjustments of 93 mixed-Korean children placed in American homes (most of the adoptive parents were white, with a few couples being of Black ancestry). Information on adjustment was obtained from progress reports of the child welfare agencies supervising the placements, letters received from parents,

Table 27

ADOPTIVE OUTCOME STUDIES

Study and Date	Size of Study Group and Lapse of Time Between Placement and Study	Outcome		Date Used for Follow-Up Assessment	Auspices
		Number and Percentages	Outcome Criteria for Categorization		
Theis (1924)	235 (adults 12-18 years after placement	207 (88.1%) 28 (11.9%)	"Capable" "Incapable"	Interviews with adoptive parents, and "other persons" by project interviewer	Agency
Morrison (1950)	24 (children) 10-17 years after placement	18 (75%) 6 (25%)	"Getting along satisfactorily" "Unsatisfactory adjustment"	Interviews with adoptive parents by agency workers	Agency
Brenner (1951)	50 (families) median of 4.4 years after placement	26 (52%) 18 (36%) 6 (12%)	"Successful" "Fairly successful" "Unsuccessful"	Observation of children in home, interviews with adoptive mothers by agency workers, psychological tests of children	Agency
Nieden (1951)	138 (adults) 15-20 years after placement	35 (25%) 62 (45%) 29 (21%) 12 (9%)	"Very good" "Good" "Indifferent" "Bad"	Records and interviews with adoptive parents by agency social workers	Agency
Armatruda (1951)	100 (children) at time of placement	76 (76%) 16 (16%) 8 (8%)	"Good" "Questionable" "Poor"	Agency study of adoptive home, study of child by Yale development clinic	Agency
Armatruda (1951)	100 (children) at time of placement	46 (46%) 26 (25%) 28 (28%)	"Good" "Questionable" "Poor"	Agency study of adoptive home, study of child by Yale development clinic	Independent

Table 27 (Continued)

Study and Date	Size of Study Group and Lapse of Time Between Placement and Study	Outcome		Date Used for Follow-Up Assessment	Auspices
		Number and Percentages	Outcome Criteria for Categorization		
Fairwether (1952)	18 (children) 3-4 years after placement	18 (100%)	"Good"	Interviews with adoptive mothers by agency workers, psychological tests of children	Agency
Edwards (1954)	79 (children) 5 years after placement	69 (87%) 9 (12%) 1 (1%)	"Very happy" "Some problems" "Serious problems"	Information not available	Agency
National Association for Mental Health, England (Estimated 1954)	163 (children) minimum of 2 years after placement	142 (87.1%) 21 (12.9%)	"Satisfactory" "Unsatisfactory"	Agency records	Agency
Davis and Douck (1955)	396 (children) 1 year after placement	371 (93.7%) 25 (6.3%)	Not removed Removed	Agency records	Agency
Fradkin and Krugman (1956)	37 (children) during first year after placement	27 (73%) 6 (16%) 4 (11%)	"Good" "Intermediate" "Poor"	Ongoing contact with parents during first year of supervision tests of infant	Agency
Witmer et al. (1963)	484 (children) most 9 years after placement	324 (67%) 39 (8%) 121 (25%)	"Excellent to fair" "Not definitely unsatisfactory" "Definitely unsatisfactory"	Interviews with parents and teachers by project interviewers, psychological test of children	Agency

Table 27 (Concluded)

Outcome	Number	Percent
Unequivocally successful	1,421	78
"Fairly successful" "Indifferent" "Questionable" "Some problems" "Intermediate"	143	8
"Unsatisfactory" "Poor" "Problematic" "Unsuccessful" "Incapable"	260	14
Total	1,824	100

Source: Child Welfare Services by Alfred Kadushin, New York: Macmillian Co., 1967, pp. 482-483. Permission for reproducing table was received from the author.

and conversations with local adoption workers. The length of time the children had been in their adoptive homes ranged from a few months to nearly two years. During the first few days following placement the children usually were apprehensive and bewildered, with various adjustment problems being noted, particularly among the children who were older. With passage of time, adjustment problems subsided with the author concluding,

> ... the difficulties experienced by children and parents alike are to be expected and remain within normal limits, while the happiness of both seems as satisfying as in any local adoption placements. (p. 5)

The writer is unaware of later follow-up studies conducted on the outcome of placing Korean children with American couples. Buck (1965) and Issac (1965) indicate their impressions derived from personal experience in this field are that the outcome is generally quite successful.

DiVirgilis (1956) reported on the initial adjustments of twenty-four foreign born children (8 of which were Oriental) to being placed for adoption with an American family. The author notes there generally were no attempts to match the coloring of the child to the parents. Some initial adjustment problems are mentioned, but after the first few months adjustment difficulties are reported to have been resolved satisfactorily.

Nordlie and Reed (1962) asked adoption workers to fill out a questionnaire on the post-adoptive adjustment of children who had been referred, prior to placement, to a genetics consultant to make a determination of the mixed racial background. Follow-up information was obtained on thirty-two such children who were adopted. Some of these children were reported to be of mixed-Black ancestry. Adjustment was rated as "good" in twenty-eight cases (88%), "questionable" in two (6%), and "not good" in two (6%) (p. 304). The length of time between placement and rating outcome was not specified.

The methodology of the studies cited above on the outcome of transracial adoptions, as the reader will note, has not been very rigorous. Fortunately, a more in-depth and scientifically acceptable study is presently being completed by Fanshel (1964), in cooperation with the Child Welfare League of America and the U.S. Bureau of Indian Affairs. The project is a longitudinal outcome study of 100 white couples who adopted an Indian child. The study design includes a series of interviews with the adoptive couples. In a preliminary report of the initial findings, Fanshel (1966) concludes,

In reviewing the first sequence of interviews with these parents, one is left with the overall impression that the first few years of the living experience with these adoptions have proven to be uneventful in the sense that the children seem well integrated in their families and very few signs of rejection or severe emotional disturbance have emerged in the early period. Perhaps this might be labeled the "honeymoon" period, and one should not expect that the sample of children will continue to be as problem-free when they are of an older age. However, the same thing might be said about white children living with their own families. It would be unreal to expect that out of one hundred children there would not be a few who subsequently develop middle-range and perhaps even serious problems. (p. 20)

Falk's (1970) study contained two items in his questionnaire which related to the adoptive parents' overall level of satisfaction. (As mentioned earlier the study contained two groups, an intraracial group and a group of white parents who adopted either a Black or an Indian child.) In response to questionnaire items, transracial adoptive couples were found to be less likely to indicate adoptive couples could feel as loving to an adopted child as to a genetic child; and were less affirmative in response to a question regarding whether they would adopt if they had a choice of repeating the experience. (These findings will be reviewed in greater detail in a later section of this chapter.)

Parents' Own Rating of Outcome

The outcome criterion used in this study, as described in Chapter 2, is parental satisfaction with adoptive experience. One of the ways to apply this criterion is to simply ask the adoptive couples to rate their overall satisfaction with the adoptive experience.

After the adoptive couples had responded to the interview questions, they were asked to fill out a form containing questions relating to their adoptive experiences; one of the questions asked was:

Check the one phrase on the following scale which best expresses your overall feeling about your adoptive experience with (name of child).

Looking back over the whole experience with (   ), I feel it has been:

_____ Extremely satisfying

_____ More satisfying than dissatisfying

_____ About half and half

_____ More dissatisfying than satisfying

_____ Extremely dissatisfying

The distribution of the responses to this question is displayed in Table 28.

Table 28

ADOPTIVE PARENTS' RATING OF LEVEL OF SATISFACTION WITH
OVERALL ADOPTIVE EXPERIENCE

Study Group	Response	No. of TRA Fathers	No. of TRA Mothers	Total No.	Percent
TRA Parents	Extremely satisfying	36	36	72	88
	More satisfying than dissatisfying	5	4	9	11
	About half and half		1	1	1
	More dissatisfying than satisfying				--
	Extremely dissatisfying				--
	Total	41	41	82	100

Study Group	Response	No. of IRA Fathers	No. of IRA Mothers	Total No.	Percent
IRA Parents	Extremely satisfying	39	39	78	95
	More satisfying than dissatisfying	2	2	4	5
	About half and half				--
	More dissatisfying than satisfying				--
	Extremely dissatisfying				
	Total	41	41	82	100

Note: The results of Wilcoxon matched-pairs signed-ranks tests for data shown on Tables 28, 30, 32, 34, and 35 are presented in Appendix N.

One of the notable features of these results is the high rating assigned by both TRA and IRA couples to overall satisfaction with the adoptive experience. In addition, a Wilcoxon matched-pairs signed-ranks test of differences between the ratings by TRA and IRA couples was not significant.

Categorizing the success of an adoption on the basis of these satisfaction categories is somewhat arbitrary. One way of making such a categorization is to consider the ratings of "Extremely satisfying" and "More satisfying than dissatisfying" as representing a successful outcome. Using such a classification, the results show 81 of the 82 (99%) TRA parents, and all of the IRA parents regard their adoption as being successful.

This high rate of success for both groups is considerably higher than the average success rate in prior outcome studies; including outcome studies on intraracial adoptions (as indicated in Table 27). One explanation that might be suggested for this high rate of success is that parents may be apt to rate the outcome as being more satisfying than other methods of determining parental satisfaction.

Such an explanation, however, would seem to be discredited by Kadushin's (1966) study of ninety-one couples who adopted older children (five years of age and older). In that study the parents also rated their overall satisfaction with the adoptive experience on a checklist form (the question was identical to the one used in this study). The distribution of the responses is shown in Table 29.

Table 29

RESULTS OF KADUSHIN'S (1966) STUDY OF PARENTS' OWN RATING OF LEVEL OF
SATISFACTION WITH OVERALL ADOPTIVE EXPERIENCE

Level of Satisfaction	Number of Parents	Percent
Extremely satisfying	110	60
More satisfying than dissatisfying	33	18
About half and half	12	7
More dissatisfying than satisfying	8	4
Extremely dissatisfying	3	2
Now answered	16	9
Total	182	100

Kadushin (1966) reports that these ratings by parents were closely associated with other measures of parental satisfaction used in the study, such as the ratio of satisfactions-to-dissatisfactions expressed during the interviews. A comparison, however, of Table 28 and Table 29 show that both the IRA and TRA parents tended to assign a substantially higher rating to satisfaction with the overall outcome than the parents in Kadushin's study. Excluding the "not answered" tallies from Kadushin's results, a Kolmogorov-Smirnov test of differences in ratings between the parents in Kadushin's study and the TRA parents in this study was significant (two-tailed), .05 level;[*] with the TRA parents being more likely to assign higher ratings.

Further support for the notion that the high success rate found in this study is not a function of the parents being more likely to assign a higher rating is provided by the interviewer's impression of the parents' overall satisfaction with the adoptive experience. After asking the interview questions, the interviewers rated the overall parental satisfactions according to the following instructions:

While the parents are filling out the questionnaire, check (for each parent) the phrase on the following scale which best expresses your impression of how satisfying each parent feels his/her adoptive experience with _____ (CHILD) has been:

---

[*] Note: The results of Kolmogorov-Smirnov test for data shown in Tables 28 and 29 are presented in Appendix O.

	MOTHER		FATHER
_____	Extremely satisfying	_____	Extremely satisfying
_____	More satisfying than dissatisfying	_____	More satisfying than dissatisfying
_____	About half and half	_____	About half and half
_____	More dissatisfying than satisfying	_____	More dissatisfying than satisfying
_____	Extremely dissatisfying	_____	Extremely dissatisfying

Before presenting the results, it should be noted the accuracy with which interviewers are able to determine the overall level of parental satisfaction after only one interview is open to question. Furthermore, it should be pointed out that only the researcher (who interviewed approximately one-fourth of the families) holds a Master's Degree in social work. The other four interviewers, although having had prior training and experience in interviewing, have had limited formal training in diagnostic assessment of personal feelings.

This measure, then, can at best be considered a "soft" measure of parental satisfaction. The distribution of the ratings is shown in Table 30.

Table 30

INTERVIEWERS' RATINGS OF ADOPTIVE PARENTS' OVERALL LEVEL OF
SATISFACTION WITH ADOPTIVE EXPERIENCE

Study Group	Response	No. of TRA Fathers	No. of TRA Mothers	Total No.	Percent
TRA Parents	Extremely satisfying	36	38	74	90
	More satisfying than dissatisfying	4	3	7	9
	About half and half	1		1	1
	More dissatisfying than satisfying				
	Extremely dissatisfying	—	—	—	—
	Total	41	41	82	100

Study Group	Response	No. of IRA Fathers	No. of IRA Mothers	Total No.	Percent
IRA Parents	Extremely satisfying	39	39	78	95
	More satisfying than dissatisfying	2	1	3	4
	About half and half		1	1	1
	More dissatisfying than satisfying	--	--	--	--
	Extremely dissatisfying	—	—	—	—
	Total	41	41	82	100

It should be noted the interviewers were instructed to rate the outcome while the parents were filling out the checklist form , and therefore before seeing the parents' ratings of overall adoption satisfaction. A Wilcoxon matched-pairs signed-ranks test of differences in interviewer's ratings between IRA and TRA couples was not significant.

A comparison of Table 28 and Table 30 shows the distribution of the satisfaction ratings by interviewers and by the adoptive parents are amazingly consistent. A Spearman's rank order correlation between the parents' own rating and the interviewers' rating of overall satisfaction was r = 91. The interviewers' ratings being consistent with the parents own ratings provides confirmatory support for the higher than anticipated success ratings for both study groups.

Another explanation for the high ratings is that the first few years following placement are a "honeymoon" period, and that more dissatisfactions will develop with passage of time as the child grows older. Such an argument has been advanced by Kornitzer (1968) ,

The first few years of an adoption, when the child arrives as a baby, are the honeymoon period, years of relative security in which the relationship is not yet subjected to the sanctions and stresses of the outside world. This honeymoon may well last until the child first goes to school; in many cases the child has not been told he is adopted, so that the adoption has not yet been "proved." Until school age, therefore, no useful assessment of the success of failure of the adoption can be made. (p. 158)

There may be some truth in Kornitzer's assertion. However, as Table 27 shows, other outcome studies (by Armatruda, 1951; National Association for Mental Health; Davis & Douck, 1955; and Fradkin & Krugman, 1956) have been conducted within the first few years after placement. In addition, Jersild's (1949) extensive study of joys and problems in child rearing, found almost as many problems and dissatisfactions reported among parents with children in the 0-4 age group as among parents with children in older age groups (p. 78).

When applied to transracial adoptions, Kornitzer's argument is further weakened. Kornitzer's main point is that the relationship between the adopted child and the adoptive parents is not likely to be "subjected to the sanctions and stresses of the outside world" (p. 158) until the child is of school age. However, as noted in the previous chapter, adoptive parents of a Black child are likely to receive the strongest opposition and "sanctions" from relatives, friends, and neighbors when first informed about the adoption, with the reactions of such people generally becoming more favorable with the passage of time.

Switching the focus, somewhat, the main question at issue appears to be, "Are such high success rates as reported in this study higher than what might be expected?" Perhaps they are. However, there are several reasons to expect the parents in this study would generally be satisfied with their child. First of all, these parents wanted a child, and went through a long-involved agency review process. The adoptive study supposedly weeded out "unsuitable" applicants, and also aided approved applicants in closely examining probable future rewards and problems. The generally high educational level of the parents in the study group should further have assisted them in taking a look at the future, and in arriving at a rational decision over whether adopting a child is likely to be a personally satisfying experience for them. Not only were such adoptive parents motivated and given substantial preparation for the adoption, they also were given some choice in the type of child selected (e.g., age, sex, race,

73

background). Most of the TRA parents also had other children in the family, which should have further enabled them to be aware of future satisfactions and problems, and arrive at a rational decision regarding whether it is in their family's best interest to adopt. As noted in Chapter II in the description of the procedures for the selection of the study group, several of the IRA couples refused to participate in this study, and were therefore replaced by other IRA couples. It is possible that some of the IRA couples who refused to participate were somewhat dissatisfied with their adoption, and may have refused because they either did not want to face this dissatisfaction during an interview, or did not want anyone else to become aware of their dissatisfaction. Inclusion of the IRA couples who refused to participate may therefore have reduced slightly the high overall success rate found for the IRA couples.

The main conclusion, however, to be derived from the adoptive parents' own rating of overall satisfaction were the adoptive experience is: high ratings were reported by both groups, with a Wilcoxon matched-pairs signed-ranks test showing the differences in ratings between the IRA and TRA couples were insignificant.

Instrument Assessment of Outcome

Another method of measuring the overall level of parental satisfaction is to have the parents rate their degree of satisfaction with a number of specific aspects of the adoptive experience. The underlying assumption is that overall satisfaction is a composite of specific satisfactions and dissatisfactions with the adoptive experience.

In a comparison field, measuring marital success, a number of marital satisfaction instruments have been developed, based on the similar assumption that general satisfaction with one's marriage is a composite of specific satisfactions and dissatisfactions; (Terman, 1938; Burgess & Cottrell, 1939; Locke, 1951; Burgess & Wallin, 1953; Locke & Wallace, 1959, and Most, 1964). A high degree of reliability and validity has been reported for a number of these tests (Bowerman, 1964).

The Adoption Satisfaction Scale developed for this study is presented in Table 31. The schedule asks the parents to rate their degree of satisfaction with certain behavioral, physical, and personality characteristics of the child; and with the child's relationship with both parents. The last two questions in the schedule were designed to obtain an indirect rating of the general satisfaction with the adoptive experience.

The study group parents were requested to fill out this schedule after the interview was completed. Before giving the schedule to the parents, the interviewer informed the parents the schedule was not a test, and also asked the parents to refrain from comparing or discussing their answers while filling out the schedule.

For the first 22 items, a four-point weight scale was used for each item (ranging from one point being assigned for "Very dissatisfied" to four points for "Very satisfied"). For the final two questions, a five point scale was used (ranging from one point for "Definitely no" to five points for "Definitely yes"). The possible total score on the schedule ranged from a minimum of 24 points to a maximum of 98 points.

The mean scores and range of scores achieved by TRA and IRA parents are presented in Table 32.

Table 31

ADOPTION SATISFACTION SCALE

This is not any kind of a test. When it comes to family life and adoption there are not "Right" or "Wrong" answers. Your attitude or opinion about each question is "Right" for you, and you should answer it that way.

The questions that follow can all be answered by putting a check mark (√) in the appropriate place. Please be sure to answer every question.

Rate the degree of your satisfaction with your adopted child in the following respects:

	Very Satisfied	Moderately Satisfied	Somewhat Dissatisfied	Very Dissatisfied
Eating habits				
Sleeping habits				
Bladder control				
Cleanliness habits				
Affectional responses				
Physical health				
Obedience				
Control of temper				
Personality				
Speech development				
Ease at which child to others				
Rate of learning				
Play activities				
Interests--skills				
Mood--disposition				
Physical appearance				
Attention demands				
Ease at which child adjusted to your spouse following placement				
Child's relationship with your spouse				
Child's relationship with you				
Amount of time needed to care for child				

For each of the next two questions, check the box on the scale line which indicates your response. The scale gradually ranges on one side from Definitely No, to Definitely Yes on the other side.

75

Table 31 (Concluded)

1. Do you think parents are apt to feel as loving toward their adopted child as toward a natural child?

_____

| Definitely No | Somewhat uncertain, but probably No | Uncertain | Somewhat uncertain, but probably Yes | Definitely Yes |

2. If you had to do it over again, would you adopt this child?

_____

| Definitely No | Somewhat uncertain, but probably No | Uncertain | Somewhat uncertain, but probably Yes | Definitely Yes |

Table 32

MEAN SCORES AND RANGE OF SCORES OBTAINED BY ADOPTIVE PARENTS
ON ADOPTION SATISFACTION SCALE

Parents	Mean Score	Range of Scores
TRA Wives (N = 41)	92.1	72-98
TRA Husbands (N = 41)	92.1	77-98
IRA Wives (N = 41)	92.2	85-98
IRA Husbands (N = 41)	91.9	95-98

The mean scores achieved by the study group parents on the Adoption Satisfaction Scale reveal three findings worthy of note. The mean scores for the IRA and TRA parents (presented by sex) are amazingly consistent for the four subgroups; which suggests the overall level of satisfaction with adoption experience is similar for all subgroups. With almost identical mean scores, it is not surprising that a Wilcoxon matched-pairs signed-ranks test of differences in satisfaction scores between TRA and IRA couples, was not significant.

The second item worthy of note is the high level of the mean scores for the four subgroups. (As indicated earlier, the range of possible scores on the schedule was from 24 to 98.) The high mean scores indicate a high degree of satisfaction with the adoptive experience. *

_____

*The high mean scores on the Adoption Satisfaction Scale have been interpreted in this analysis as indicating both study groups have a high degree of satisfaction with their adoptive experience. Although this interpretation is consistent with the parents' own ratings and the interviewers' ratings of the parents' overall satisfaction, another interpretation is possible. The reliability and validity of the instrument were not examined in this study, and therefore it is possible that the test may not be able to measure differences in satisfaction with adoptive experience; e.g., as would be consistent with the results of this study, every other group of adoptive parents taking the test may score in the same high range as the two groups in this study. To use a familiar but appropriate cliche, it would be desirable for future research to ascertain the reliability and validity of this instrument.

The third item worthy of note is that these results are consistent with the findings in the previous section on the adopters' own rating of satisfaction with adoption experience:

a)   IRA and TRA parents assign a high rating to overall satisfaction with adoptive experience.

b)   No significant differences were found between IRA and TRA couples in overall satisfaction with adoptive experience.

Review of Falk's Outcome Findings

Falk (1968) asked the following two questions related to parental satisfaction, with the intraracial and transracial couples being asked to respond on a seven point scale; with the scale ranging from "strongly disagree" (one-point) to "strongly agree" (seven-points):

a)   Do you think that parents can feel as loving toward their adopted children as toward their natural children? (p. 55)

b)   If you had it to do over again, would you adopt a child? ("of another or mixed race" is added to the TRA questionnaire) (p. 56)

Falk (1970) found significantly higher mean scores for the intraracial parents in response to both of these questions, and proceeds to conclude, "Taken together, the responses indicated somewhat less satisfaction with transracial adoption than with intraracial adoptions" (p. 88). Such a conclusion suggests transracial adoptions are less successful than intraracial adoptions, and perhaps even raises a question whether transracial adoptions should be promoted. Because of the important implications, a second look will be taken of Falk's findings.

Falk's findings, of course, are inconsistent with this study's more involved assessment of parental satisfaction.

In addition, it should be noted Falk's transracial group was composed of white couples who adopted children of various minority races; primarily children of either Indian or Black ancestry.

The mean scores to Falk's two questions are presented in Table 33 for three groups of parents: intraracial, adoptive parents of a Black child, and adoptive parents of an Indian child.

There are two noteworthy features of these mean scores. One is the high level of the scores; on a scale of 7, all of the mean scores are above 6.5. Such high mean scores imply a high level of parental satisfaction by all three groups of parents, which may well be the most important finding to be derived from these results.

The second is that, in comparing the mean scores of the parents of a Black child to the scores of the parents of an Indian child, the mean scores of the parents of a Black child are lower for question (a), but higher for question (b). In fact, the mean scores for question (b) by the adoptive parents of a Black child are very close to the scores for the intraracial group.

Falk's statistical tests for differences combined the two transracial groups, and did not directly test for differences between intraracial parents and adoptive parents

Table 33

FALK'S (1968) DATA ON MEAN SCORES OF RESPONSES BY INTRARACIAL AND
TRANSRACIAL PARENTS TO QUESTIONS RELATED TO PARENTAL SATISFACTION

| | Mean Score | | | | | |
| | Intraracial Parents | | Adoptive Parents of a Black Child | | Adoptive Parents of an Indian Child | |
	Husband (N = 168)	Wife (N = 170)	Husband (N = 59)	Wife (N = 59)	Husband (N = 90)	Wife (N = 90)
Question A. "Ability to feel as loving to adopted child"	6.893	6.935	6.644	6.593	6.789	6.811
Question B. "Desire to repeat adoption"	6.851	6.894	6.763	6.830	6.689	6.733

of a Black child. Unfortunately, Falk (1968) does not provide the standard deviations for these groups, which would have permitted a direct test of differences of means between intraracial parents and adoptive parents of a Black child. However, the reported mean scores suggest there is apt to be a statistical difference in responses to the first question, but perhaps no significant difference in responses to the second question.

The present study provides some additional information in regards to Falk's two questions. The last two questions in the Adoption Satisfaction Scale were adapted from Falk's two questions, with the wording being very similar. The distribution of the responses of the IRA and TRA parents to these two questions are presented in Tables 34 and 35.

A Wilcoxon matched-pairs signed-ranks test of differences between IRA and TRA parents (two-tailed, .05 level) was insignificant for the question regarding "repeating the experience"; but significant for the question of "ability to feel as loving toward adopted child as toward a genetic child." Such results are consistent with the general direction of Falk's findings.

Even though the findings in this study indicate TRA parents do not differ significantly from IRA parents in overall level of parental satisfaction, they apparently are less likely to be as affirmative in their response to a question regarding ability to feel as loving toward an adopted child. The reasons for this latter finding are not known. One explanation is the difference may be related to the finding that TRA parents were more likely to have natural born children. Shaw (1953) in a follow-up study found many of the parents who had genetic children reported a difference in quality (but not in quantity) of their love towards natural and adopted children. Since the TRA parents in this study were more apt to have genetic children, they may have been more likely to feel a qualitative difference in love towards the adopted child, and therefore have assigned a slightly lower rating to this question. (Again, it perhaps is worthwhile to reiterate the differences between TRA and IRA parents in their responses to this question were slight, with parents in both groups generally being very affirmative in their responses.)

78

Table 34

ADOPTIVE PARENTS' ATTITUDES TOWARD ABILITY TO FEEL AS LOVING
TOWARD ADOPTED CHILD AS TOWARD GENETIC CHILD

Study Group	Response	No. of TRA Fathers	No. of TRA Mothers	Total No.	Percent
TRA Parents	Definitely yes	36	36	72	88
	Somewhat uncertain, but probably yes	4	5	9	11
	Uncertain	1		1	1
	Somewhat uncertain, but probably no				
	Definitely no				
	Totals	41	41	82	100

Study Group	Response	No. of IRA Fathers	No. of IRA Mothers	Total No.	Percent
IRA Parents	Definitely yes	39	41	80	98
	Somewhat uncertain, but probably yes	2	--	2	2
	Uncertain				
	Somewhat uncertain, but probably no				
	Definitely no				
	Totals	41	41	82	100

Table 35

ADOPTIVE PARENTS' RESPONSES TO QUESTION REGARDING REPEATING THE EXPERIENCE

Study Group	Response	No. of TRA Fathers	No. of TRA Mothers	Total No.	Percent
TRA Parents	Definitely yes	38	40	78	95
	Somewhat uncertain, but probably yes	3		3	4
	Uncertain		1	1	1
	Somewhat uncertain, but probably no				
	Definitely no				
	Totals	41	41	82	100

Study Group	Response	No. of IRA Fathers	No. of IRA Mothers	Total No.	Percent
IRA Parents	Definitely yes	40	41	81	99
	Somewhat uncertain, but probably yes				
	Uncertain	1		1	1
	Somewhat uncertain, but probably no				
	Definitely no				
	Totals	41	41	82	100

CHAPTER VI

SUMMARY AND CONCLUSIONS

Purpose

The purpose of this study was to investigate the outcome of placing Black children with white couples for adoption. The two more specific objectives were to: a) Identify the specific satisfactions derived and difficulties encountered by white parents who adopted a Black child, and b) Assess the overall outcome of white couples-Black children adoptions. This type of transracial placement is of recent origin, with very limited information currently available on the outcome. At the present time numerous adoption workers, judges, attorneys, and referral sources are cautious about encouraging such placements because of speculations about problems that may arise due to bringing together into a family unit members of the two polar races (black and white) in our society (Open Door Society, 1970). If this type of placement is found to have a successful outcome, such transracial placements are to be encouraged and offers hope of more fully meeting the need of finding parents for the large number of parentless Black children. The Children's Bureau recently estimated there are between 40,000 and 80,000 Black children available for adoption for whom an adoptive home cannot be found (Riday, 1969).

Study Design

Two groups of families composed the study group; a group of 44 white couples who adopted a Black child, and a matched group of white couples who adopted a child of their own race. (Three of the TRA couples were without a matched IRA pair, and therefore the data on these three couples were not included when statistical tests were conducted.) The two groups were matched on the age of the adopted child, and on the socio-economic status of the adoptive parents. Two additional requirements for inclusion in the study group were that the adoption needed to be finalized, and the child had to be no older than six years of age.

The study data on the adoptive satisfactions derived and difficulties encountered by the two groups in the study were obtained by an interview held in the home of the adoptive parents, and by reading the agency adoptive record material on these families. The outcome criterion used to determine the overall outcome was parental satisfaction with adoptive experience.

Characteristics of Families in Study Group

The TRA couples were found to be as eligible for adoptive parenthood at time of adoption as the IRA couples. In addition, the TRA couples appeared to be less likely than adoptive couples of hard-to-place children other than Black, to have marginal eligibility for adoptive parenthood.

The TRA couples were found to generally have a high socio-economic status. Since the IRA couples were matched on this factor, they also had a high status. The age differences between TRA and IRA parents at time of placement were not significant. TRA parents, however, tended to be married longer at the time of placement, were more likely to have natural-born children and to be fertile at time of placement, and more apt to reside in large urban communities.

The expressed reasons for adopting indicated IRA couples tend to adopt for parent-centered reasons; they desired children in order to complete their family, to fulfill their life and marriage, to be a companion for other children in the family, with a majority indicating they wanted to adopt because they were unable to have natural-born children. In contrast, the reasons expressed by TRA couples were more child-centered; primarily to provide a home to a child who otherwise may not be adopted. These couples generally were able to bear children; but because of the need for adoptive homes, tended to view adopting a Black child as being the first-choice method to enlarging their family. TRA couples also appeared to be concerned about social issues, such as race relations and the over-population problem; but only a few were reported to be involved in organized civil rights activities, with no incidents of militant activity being noted in the record material.

Of the adopted children in the TRA group, 18 were boys and 23 were girls; the reverse was the case for the IRA group, 23 were boys and 18 were girls. All of the children, except one, were separated from the natural parents shortly after birth. The mean age at time of placement for the TRA group was 6.0 months, and the mean age for the IRA group was 3.8 months. Most of the children in both groups had one foster home placement prior to the adoptive home placement. Very few behavioral problems were manifested by these children prior to adoptive placement as noted in the record material. No serious health problems were reported for the Black children prior to placement ; five of the white children had rather serious medical problems. The age range for the TRA children at time of follow-up interview was from 19 months to 67 months, with a mean of 34.8 months. For the IRA children the age range was from 19 months to 73 months, with a mean of 35.7 months. According to the record material, 40 of the 41 TRA children were of "mixed-Black" parentage, with only one having both natural parents classified as "Black."

Experiences of Adoptive Parents

All of the TRA and IRA parents at the time of the follow-up interview stated they had the parental feeling the adopted child was really their own; in fact, a majority of parents in both groups reported feeling the child was really their own within a few days following placement. Many of the TRA couples mentioned they became "color-blind" shortly after adopting; i.e., they stopped seeing the child as a Black, and instead came to perceive the child as an individual, an individual who is a member of their family.

One of the most notable findings is that TRA parents reported considerably fewer problems related to the race of the child have arisen than they anticipated prior to the adoption.

Thirty-nine of the 44 TRA couples reported negative responses (ranging from minor misgivings to outspoken disapproval) were received from some of their relatives when first informed about the adoption. With the passage of time, such opposition has subsided substantially; and at the time of the follow-up interview the TRA parents reported almost all of the grandparents and other relatives have come to accept the child as a member of the family. None of the TRA couples reported any of their friends or neighbors directly expressed intense disapproval of the adoption when first informed. Some neighbors, however, were reported to have expressed mild disapproval, and the TRA parents heard indirectly that some neighbors made critical comments to other people about the adoption. Many of the TRA couples reported their friends were "encouraging" and "happy for us" when first informed of the adoption. At the time of the follow-up interview, neighbors, and friends were reported, in almost all cases, to have accepted the child. As might be expected, the reactions of relatives, friends and neighbors to the IRA adoptions, when first informed, tended to be more approving and accepting than for the TRA adoptions.

Those families having other children at the time of adoption reported the adopted child has been fully accepted by the other children as siblings, with normal sibling relationships developing shortly after placement. No difficulties in acceptance of the adopted child by other children in the neighborhood were noted by either the IRA or TRA families. Only 8 TRA couples mentioned they were aware their child had been called derogatory names related to the color of the child's skin. Most of the TRA families reported no adverse reactions from strangers to the adoption; with the usual reactions being reported as curious stares, surprise, and puzzled expressions.

Satisfactions Derived and Difficulties Encountered by Transracial Parents

The TRA and IRA couples were asked several questions related to satisfactions and dissatisfactions with their adoptive experience. The ratio of expressed satisfactions to dissatisfactions for both groups was approximately 2.5:1. The satisfactions and dissatisfactions expressed by the TRA and IRA couples were quite similar, implying they are experiencing common satisfactions and dissatisfactions from adopting a child. TRA couples showed a tendency to cite more satisfactions in the area of human relations (such as seeing their Black child being accepted by white people); while IRA couples tended to mention more satisfactions in the area of parent-child relationships (this latter finding may have been due to many of the IRA couples having their first parental experience).

One of the notable dissatisfactions reported by some of the TRA and IRA couples was the "gushing" reaction (remarks such as, "What a wonderful thing you're doing in providing this child with a home"). The adoptive couples mentioned they find such comments irritating as they do not view their adoption as a charitable act; rather they feel they adopted because of anticipated personal gratifications they would receive from having a child (or another child) in their family.

The TRA couples were asked what they thought are the special satisfactions obtained by white parents who adopt a Black child. The items cited in decreasing order of frequency were: providing a home to a child who otherwise may not have a permanent family; making a positive contribution to improving race relations; none-receive same satisfactions as if child were white; is a way to live one's beliefs; verifies belief there is no difference between Blacks and whites; leads to increased insight into black culture; increases awareness of racial problems; black (mixed-race) children are physically attractive; increases sensitivity to prejudices; leads to less prejudice among our other children; leads to development of friendly relationships with Blacks.

In response to a question regarding special problems white adoptive parents of a Black child are apt to encounter, an average of about one problem per family was cited by the TRA couples. This small average suggests TRA couples, after having an adopted Black child in their home for a couple of years, believe transracial adoption presents few special problems. The items cited, in decreasing order of frequency were: helping child to understand black culture and establish an identity; helping chile (when older) to understand why he may be subjected to discrimination; criticism from relatives, neighbors and friends; reactions of white people in community who disapprove; disapproval of the adoption by some Blacks; impact of Black child on other children in family; development of special problems will depend on where family lives. The additional following 6 responses to the question were mentioned by only one (although not the same) TRA couple: inferences of unfaithfulness to spouse, handling own prejudices and stereotypes, perhaps some difficulty (by the TRA parents) in obtaining employment; receiving stares from other people; reaction of black child to being raised in a white family; anticipating more problems than will arise.

Anticipation of Future Problems

In spearate questions the TRA couples were asked if they expect their child will have any particular problems due to race in elementary school, in seeking employment, in dating, and in forming an identity. In the first two areas only a minority of the TRA couples anticipate problems due to race will arise, with the problems cited being relatively minor in nature. Eleven (25%) TRA couples reported they anticipate some problems in elementary school, with name-calling being the most frequently mentioned difficulty. Sixteen (36%) TRA couples indicate they expect some difficulty due to race will be encountered in seeking employment.

More problems, and of a more serious nature, are anticipated due to race in the areas of dating and forming an identity. Thirty-seven (84%) TRA couples expect problems will occur in the dating area. Problems cited were objections from parents of potential dates; TRA sons experiencing some refusals when arranging dates, TRA daughters being subjected to more pressure from white dates to have pre-marital relations; and the TRA person facing an identity decision over whether to date Blacks or whites.

Eighteen (41%) TRA couples mentioned they thought the child will in future years experience some identity formation problems due to race. These parents appeared to be somewhat uncertain of the specific problems that may arise, but commented the TRA person may have difficulty in deciding which race to identify with, difficulty in understanding why he is subjected to discrimination, and difficulty in deciding, "Where do I belong," and "Who am I." Ten (23%) other TRA couples mentioned they are uncertain if the TRA person will have difficulty in establishing a self-identity, with some of their comments indicating this is an area of concern. Other publications (e.g., Falk, 1968; and Open Door Society, 1970) also note difficulties a black child reared in a white home may experience in developing an identity is currently a major concern in the field of transracial adoptions.

Unfortunately there has been no decisive research on the dynamics of identity formation for TRA persons. Various outcomes of identity formation can be developed by using different theoretical concepts. This writer's personal opinion is the speculated problems have been exaggerated. The writer's view on this topic will be briefly summarized.

Socio-psychological theory suggests that if a child is given the proper guidance and affection by his parents, he will begin to develop a positive self-identity and social skills for dealing with his environment. During childhood, a TRA person will be exposed to some white people who react to him in terms of stereotypes about his race; however, with the explanations and emotional support of his parents, he should develop techniques of dealing with stereotype reactions. Exposure to black history and culture, and also perhaps contact with other Blacks, should further provide him with a fuller understanding of the meanings and values associated with the Black race. With such a preparation, a TRA person may be as capable of dealing with stereotype reactions to his race as other Black children. In addition, being reared in a white home may have several advantages. A TRA person may be better prepared to form positive relationships with white people, due to his childhood experiences in which he formed close relations with white parents and siblings, and in which he was exposed and acquired many of the values of his white parents. Since TRA parents generally have a high socio-economic status, they are also apt to encourage and assist the TRA person in obtaining a high education, which should further enable the TRA person to personally and financially find a place in society. In addition, various writers (e.g., Griffin, 1961) have noted many Blacks feel inferior to whites. This inferior feeling is part of one's identity and is likely to be conveyed to their children (Erikson, 1963). White adoptive parents are unlikely to have feelings of racial inferiority, and may thereby convey this more positive aspect of identity to their Black children.

In relation to the formation of identity, the question of which race a TRA person will identify with is frequently raised. The author wonders how important an identification in this area will loom to the TRA person, since there are so many other groups to identify with. Secondly, it appears the question of which race a TRA person will identify with has been improperly conceptualized. To identify means to take on the characteristics and goals of others as one's own. Since there is so much variation within subgroups of a race, it is almost impossible to determine the characteristics of either the white or black race. Therefore, the question of which race a TRA person will identify with probably needs rephrasing to: Will TRA persons identify with subgroups of either the black or white race? If the answer is affirmative, an interesting question is which subgroups they are likely to identify with.

Changes in Adoption Procedures Suggested by Adoptive Parents

In response to a question regarding suggestions for ways in which adoption agencies can improve their services, most of the adoptive parents indicated they were very pleased with the services received from the agency through which they adopted a child. Many, however, proceeded to mention certain aspects which were not helpful, and suggested ways in which they thought improvements could be made. The following suggestions appear worthy of consideration. It should be noted the author is not necessarily recommending these suggestions be incorporated into agency procedures, but merely informing agencies of the suggestions that were made. In almost all cases these suggestions were made by a minority of the adoptive parents; whether the majority would agree was not ascertained.

1. Increased staff commitment to transracial adoption.

2. Increased promotion of transracial adoption via television, radio and press. One of the more innovative techniques in this area has been to show pictures of children needing homes via the news media. (Mitchell, 1969).

3. Agencies should better inform transracial adoptive applicants about the experiences they are likely to encounter. Some TRA parents suggested it would be helpful for prospective transracial adoptive applicants to talk to white parents who have adopted a Black child.

4. Agencies should subsidize adoptions by low-income families.

5. Adoption practice should be based on an enabling approach rather than a diagnostic approach. The enabling approach was developed by Hagen (1969); he prefers to call the approach the "educative approach." With such an approach, the focus of the adoption worker shifts from screening out good from bad applicants, to encouraging self-examination by the adoptive applicants and to providing information as to the problems and rewards of

adoption so the couples can arrive at a decision about adopting which is consistent with their abilities and goals.

6. The length of time between placement and finalization of adoption should be shortened.

7. Adoption fees between agencies should be standardized.

8. The requirement that the religion of the natural mother be the same as that of the adoptive parents should be discontinued, as the requirement, at times, leads to delays in placement of children.

9. Agencies should offer to provide the services of an attorney.

10. Agencies should provide parents with a children's book that would be designed to help the child understand he is adopted.

Overall Success of Transracial Adoptions

The outcome criterion used in this study was parental satisfaction with adoptive experience. Two principle measures of this criterion were used: a) Having the parents rate their overall satisfaction with their adoptive experience; and b) Having the parents rate their degree of satisfaction with a number of specific aspects of the adoptive experience. The underlying assumption is that overall satisfaction is a composite of specific satisfactions and dissatisfactions with the adoptive experience. A checklist form, the Adoption Satisfaction Scale, was developed for this measure.

For the first measure the parents were asked to check on the following scale their degree of overall satisfaction:

_____ Extremely satisfying

_____ More satisfying than dissatisfying

_____ About half and half

_____ More dissatisfying than satisfying

_____ Extremely dissatisfying

The first two categories were considered to represent a successful outcome; and the study found 81 of the 82 (99%) TRA parents, and all of the IRA parents checked these two categories. A statistical test of differences between the two groups was not significant. These results suggest a high rate of successful outcome for both intraracial and transracial adoptions.

The interviewers' also rated their impressions of the parents' overall satisfaction on the same five point scale. (The interviewers' ratings were made immediately after the interview questions were asked, and before seeing the parents' ratings.) The satisfaction ratings by interviewers and by the adoptive parents were very consistent. The interviewers checked the first two categories for 81 of the 82 (99%) TRA parents, and also for 81 of the 82 IRA parents. A Spearman's rank order correlation between the parents' own ratings and interviewers' ratings was r = .91.

Additional support that the high rating of success in this study is not due to the parents being apt to rate the outcome as being more satisfying than other methods of determining parental satisfaction is provided in Kadushin's (1966) study of older children placed for adoption. The parents in that study were also asked to rate their degree of overall satisfaction (the question was identical to the one used in this study). Kadushin found the parents' ratings of own satisfaction was closely associated with other measures of parental satisfaction. A statistical test of differences between the ratings of the parents in Kadushin's study and the TRA parents in this study, found the TRA parents assigned significantly higher ratings.

The second measure used to assess overall satisfaction was the Adoption Satisfaction Scale, a checklist form in which the parents rated their degree of satisfaction with certain aspects of their adoptive experience. The possible total score on the schedule ranged from a minimum of 24 points to a maximum of 98 points. The mean score achieved by both TRA husbands and wives was 92.1; IRA husbands achieved a mean of 91.9 and IRA wives a mean of 92.2. These mean scores are almost identical, suggesting the overall level of satisfaction for these four subgroups is similar. A statistical test of differences found no significant difference in satisfaction scores between TRA and IRA couples. The second notable feature of the mean scores is there high level, indicating a high degree of overall satisfaction with the adoptive experience.

Thus, the two measures of parental satisfaction used in this study show a high level of overall satisfaction with adoptive experience by both IRA and TRA parents; with the level of satisfaction for the TRA couples being as high as for the IRA couples.

These results indicate the outcomes of transracial placements are as "successful" as for intraracial placements. Since the children in the study group were of pre-school age, the findings probably should not be generalized to the outcome for older TRA children. Socio-psychological theory, however, views the early years of life as being of paramount importance to a person's mental, social and emotional development. As noted earlier, prior studies have found parental satisfaction with child is closely associated with a healthy personality adjustment of the child (see e.g., Witmer, 1963; Wittenborn, 1957; Fanshel & Jaffe, 1965). If a child's social and emotional development is healthy during his formative years, socio-psychological theory would predict continued positive growth and development. Of course, a TRA child may be subjected to a few more stresses due to race than a white child as he grows older, but such a person would probably have to face such stresses even if reared by Black parents. The question then arises whether a parentless Black child is more likely to develop the necessary social skills to cope with such stresses if reared by Black or white adoptive parents. In discussing identity formation earlier, the writer speculated a TRA child is apt to be as well-prepared (or perhaps even better prepared) if reared by white adoptive parents.

In reference to transracial adoptions, Hagen (1970) asks the basic question "Is it appropriate and right to place a child of one race with parents of another?" (p. 23), and answers his own question with,

It is not necessary that a child and parent be of the same race. It is how a parent feels about his race and that of his child that is important. The parents' function remains the same for any child, to provide opportunity for the child to discover what the world is like, what the people are like, to find his own place in it, and to see himself and others as individual persons of worth and value. (p. 26)

This study provides evidence transracial placements are successful, indicating transracial placements are indeed a desirable form of care for the large number of parentless Black children.

BIBLIOGRAPHY

Adams, H. M. & Gallagher, U. M. (1963) "Some Facts and Observations About Illegitimacy," Children, 10, March-April.

Andrews, Roberta G. (1968) "Permanent Placement of Negro Children Through Adoption," Child Welfare, December.

Armatruda, C. & Balwin, J. (1951) "Current Adoption Practices," Journal of Pediatrics, 38, February.

Bernard, Jesse (1966) Marriage and Family Among Negroes, Englwood Cliffs, New Jersey: Prentice-Hall.

Berry, Brewton (1965) Race and Ethnic Relations, third edition, Boston: Houghton Mifflin Co.

Billingsley, Andrew & Giovannoni, Jeanne (1967) "Research Perspectives on Interracial Adoption" in Race, Research, and Reason, New York: National Association of Social Workers.

Blalock, Hubert M., Jr. (1960) Social Statistics, New York: McGraw-Hill.

Borgatta, E. & Fanshel, D. (1965) Behavioral Characteristics of Children Known to Psychiatric Outpatient Clinics, New York: Child Welfare League of America.

Bowerman, C. E. (1964) "Prediction Studies," in Handbook of Marriage and the Family, Harold Christensen (ed.), Chicago: Rand McNally.

Brenner, Ruth (1951) "A Follow-Up Study of Adoptive Families," Child Adoption Research Committee, March.

Brown, C. E. (1958) "The Adjustment of Adopted Children Within Their Families and in the School Environment," Thesis, Glasgow University.

Buck, Pearl (1965) Children for Adoption, New York: Random House.

Bureau of the Census (1970) Statistical Abstract of the United States, 1970, Washington, D.C.: Government Printing Office.

Burgess, E. W. & Cottrell, L. S., Jr. (1939) Predicting Success or Failure in Marriage, New York: Prentice Hall.

Burgess, E. W. & Wallin, P. (1953) Engagement and Marriage, Chicago: J. B. Lippincott.

Chambers, Donald (1970) "Willingness to Adopt Atypical Children," Child Welfare, 49, May.

Child Welfare League of America (1960) Adoption of Oriental Children by American White Families--an Interdisciplinary Symposium, New York: Child Welfare League of America.

Child Welfare League of America (1968) Standards for Adoption Service, revised, New York: Child Welfare League of America.

Child Welfare Statistics (1968) "Adoptions in 1968," U.S. Department of Health, Education, and Welfare.

Citizens' Committee for Children of New York (1963) Public Welfare: Myth vs. Fact, New York.

Clark, Sally R. (1970) "But Our Daughter Is One," Christian Herald, August.

Colvin, Ralph (1962) "Toward the Development of a Foster Parent Attitude Test," in Quantitative Approaches to Parent Selection, New York: Child Welfare League of America.

Cronbach, Lee J. (1960) Essentials of Psychological Testing, second ed., New York: Harper and Row.

Cullough, Vern (1964) "The Quiet Revolution in Adoption" The Progressive, September.

Daugherty, M. W., et al. (1958) "Achieving Adoption for Sixty Negro Children," Child Welfare, 37, October.

Davis, Ruth & Douck, Polly (1955) "Crucial Importance of Adoption Home Study," Child Welfare, 34, March.

Deasy, L. C. & Mullaney, J. W. (1970) "The Suburban White and the Adoption of Children," Social Service Review, 44, September.

Detroit News (1964) February 23 (article about the number of Negro children available for adoption in the city).

DiVirgilio, Letitia (1956) "Adjustment of Foreign Children in Their Adoptive Homes," Child Welfare, 35, November.

Edgar, Margaret (ed.) "Some Experiences in Inter-Racial Adoption," an unpublished report of transracial adoptions by the Open Door Society of Montreal.

Edwards, Jane (1961) "The Hard-to-Place Child," Child Welfare, 40, April.

Edwards, M.E. (1954) "Failure and Success in the Adoption of Toddlers," Case Conference, November.

Ehrlich, Paul R. & Holm, Richard W. (1964) "A Biological iew of Race," in The Concept of Race, Ashley Montagu (ed.), New York: The Free Press of Glencoe.

Erikson, Erik H. (1963) Childhood and Society, second ed., New York: W. W. Norton.

Fairweather, O. E. (1952) "Early Placement in Adoption," Child Welfare, 31.

Falk, Laurence L. (1968) "Trans-Racial Adoption: A Comparative Study," Mimeographed Report.

Falk, Laurence L. (1970) "A Comparative Study of Transracial and Intraracial Adoption," Child Welfare, 49, February.

Fanshel, David (1957) A Study in Negro Adoption, New York: Child Welfare League of America.

Fanshel, David (1964) "Indian Adoption Research Project," Child Welfare, 43, November.

Fanshel, David (1966) "The Indian Adoption Research Project: A Preliminary Report," paper presented at the Mid-West Regional Conference, Child Welfare League of America, Omaha, Nebraska.

Fanshel, David & Jaffe, Benson (1965) "A Follow-Up Study of Adoption--Preliminary Report," (Mimeographed).

Farmer, James (1968) "The Plight of Negro Children in America Today," Child Welfare, November.

Fishman, Joshua A. (1967) "Childhood Indoctrination for Minority-Group Membership," in Minorities in a Changing World, Milton L. Barron (ed.), New York: Arnold A. Knopf.

Fradkin, H. & Krugman D. (1956) "A Program of Adoptive Placement for Infants Under 3 Months," American Journal of Orthopyschiatry, 26.

Fricke, Harriet (1965) "Interracial Adoption: The Little Revolution," Social Work, 10, July.

Friedlander, W. A. (1968) Introduction to Social Welfare, third ed., Englewood Cliffs, New Jersey: Prentice-Hall.

Gardner, James (1969) "A Look at Families Adopting Transracially," Children's Service Society of Wisconsin (Mimeographed Report).

Graham, Lloyd (1957) "Children from Japan in American Adoptive Homes," Casework Papers, New York: Family Service Association of America.

Griffin, John (1961), Black Like Me, Boston: Houghton Mifflin.

Grossack, Martin M. (1965) "Group Belongingness Among Negroes," in Minority Groups, Arnold Rose and Caroline Rose (eds.), New York: Harper and Row.

Grow, Lucille J. (1970) A New Look at Supply and Demand in Adoption, New York: Child Welfare League of America.

Hagen, Clayton H. (1966) "Interracial Adoption," paper presented to the Human Relations Council of Bloomington, Minnesota.

Hagen, Clayton H. (1967) "Community Challenge," (Mimeographed paper).

Hagen, Clayton H. (1967) "Is the Hard-to-Place Child So Hard to Place," paper presented at Child Welfare League Midwest Conference, Des Moines, Iowa.

Hagen, Clayton H. (1969) "New Patterns in Adoption," (Mimeographed paper).

Hagen, Clayton H. (1970) "Matching Values" in Mixed Race Adoptions, Montreal: Open Door Society.

Haring, Douglass G. (1962) "Racial Differences and Human Resemblances" in American Minorities, Milton L. Barron (ed.), New York: Alfred A. Knopf.

Hawkins, Mildred (1960) "Negro Adoptions--Challenge Accepted," Child Welfare, 39, December.

Hays, William L. (1963) Statistics for Psychologists, New York: Holt.

Herzog, Elizabeth (1964) "Unwed Motherhood: Personal and Social Consequences," Welfare in Review, August.

Herzog, Elizabeth & Bernstein, Rose (1965) "Why So Few Negro Adoptions?," Children, 12, January-February.

Husbands, Ann (1970) "The Developmental Task of the Black Foster Child," Social Casework, July.

Hylton, Lydia (1965) "Trends in Adoption," Child Welfare, 44, July.

Issac, Rael Jean (1965) Adopting a Child Today, New York: Harper and Row.

Jersild, Arthur T., et al. (1949) Joys and Problems of Child Rearing, New York: Columbia University.

Kadushin, Alfred (1958) "The Legally Adoptable, Unadopted Child," Child Welfare, 37, December.

Kadushin, Alfred (1962) "A Study of Adoptive Parents of Hard-to-Place Children," Social Casework, 43, May.

Kadushin, Alfred (1966) "Adopted When Older," (Mimeographed study).

Kadushin, Alfred (1967) Child Welfare Services, New York: Macmillan Co.

Kadushin, Alfred (1967) "Reversibility of Trauma: A Follow-Up Study of Children Adopted When Older," Social Work, 12.

Kahl, J. A. & Davis, J. A. (1955) "A Comparison of Indexes of Socio-Economic Status," American Sociological Review, 20.

Kirk, David H. (1964) Shared Fate, New York: Free Press of Glencoe.

Kornitzer, Margaret (1968) Adoption and Family Life, London: Putnam.

Lebo, J. et al. (1965) "Adoptive Placement of the Negro-Caucasian Child" Master's Thesis, University of Minnesota, Minneapolis.

Locke, H. J. (1951) Predicting Adjustment in Marriage: A Comparison of a Divorced and a Happily Married Group, New York: Henry Holt.

Locke, H. J. & Wallace, K. M. (1959) "Short Marital-Adjustment and Prediction Tests: Their Reliability and Validity," Marriage and Family Living.

Maas, Henry (1960) "The Successful Adoptive Parent Applicant," Social Work, 5.

Maas, Henry S. & Engler, Richard E., Jr. (1959) Children in Need of Parents, New York: Columbia University Press.

Manning, Seaton W. (1964) "The Changing Negro Family: Implications for the Adoption of Children," Child Welfare, 43, November.

Marden, Charles & Meyer, Gladys (1962) Minorities in American Society, New York: American Book Co.

Marmor, Judd (1964) "Some Psychodynamic Aspects of Trans-Racial Adoptions," Social Work Practice.

McCoy, Jacqueline (1961) "Identity as a Factor in the Adoptive Placement of the Older Child," Child Welfare, 40, September.

McCrea, Muriel, D. (1967) "Summary of Experiences and Convictions Around Mixed Race Placements by Children's Service Centre, Montreal, Quebec," (Mimeographed paper).

Miller, D. C. (1964) Handbook of Research Design and Social Measurement, New York: David McKay.

Miller, Roger R. (ed.) (1967) Race, Research, and Reason, New York: National Association of Social Workers.

Mitchell, Marion M. (1969) "Transracial Adoptions: Philosophy and Practice," Child Welfare, 48, December.

Montagu, Ashley (1964) The Concept of Race, Ashley Montagu (ed.), New York: Free Press of Glencoe.

Morrison, Hazel (1950) "Research Study in Adoption," Child Welfare, 29.

Most, E. (1964) "Measuring Change in Marital Satisfaction," Social Work, July.

Moynihan, Daviel P. (1965) The Negro Family: The Case for National Action, U.S. Department of Labor.

National Association for Mental Health, England, A Survey Based on Adoption Case Reviews, London: NAMH, n.d.

Nemovicher, J. (1959) "A Comparative Study of Adopted Boys and Non-Adopted Boys in Respect of Specific Personality Characteristics," Doctoral dissertation, New York University.

Nieden, Margarete Z. (1951) "The Influence of Constitution and Environment Upon the Development of Adopted Children," Journal of Psychology, 31.

Nordlie, Esther & Reed, Sheldon (1962) "Follow-Up on Adoption Counseling for Children of Possible Racial Admixture," Child Welfare, 41, September.

Open Door Society (1968) "Historical Sketch of Interracial Placement Programme of Children's Service Centre, Montreal, and Formation of Open Door Society," (Mimeographed paper available through Open Door Society, Montreal, Canada).

Open Door Society (1970) Mixed Race Adoptions, Montreal: Open Door Society.

Opportunity (1970) "Adoption of Black Children in 1969," Opportunity, 6, July-August.

Perry, M. (1958) "An Experiment in Recruitment of Negro Adoptive Homes," Social Casework, 37, May.

Petit, Lois (1960) "Some Observations on the Negro Culture in the U.S.," Social Work, 5, July.

Pettigrew, Thomas F. (1964) A Profile of the Negro American, New York: D. Van Nostrand Co.

Pringle (1967) Adoption-Facts and Fallacies, New York: Humanities Press.

Rainwater, L. & Weinstein, K. (1960) And the Poor Get Children, Chicago: Quadrangle Books.

Richmond, Anthony H. (1954) The Colour Problem, New York: Doubleday and Co.

Riday (1969) "Supply and Demand in Adoption," Child Welfare, 48, October.

Roberts, R. W. (1966) "A Theoretical Overview of the Unwed Mother," in Unwed Mother, Robert W. Roberts (ed.) New York: Harper and Row.

Roskies, Ethel (1963) "An E ploratory Study of the Characteristics of Adoptive Parents of Mixed-Race Children in the Montreal Area," Montreal Star, October 19.

Schapiro, Michael (1956) A Study of Adoption Practice, Vol. I: Adoption Agencies and the Children They Serve, New York: Child Welfare League of America.

Schapiro, Michael (1957) A Study of Adoption , Vol. III: Adoption of Children with Special Needs, New York: Child Welfare League of America, pril.

Schur, E. M. (1965) Crimes Without Victims: Deviant Behavior and Public Policy, Englewood Cliffs, New Jersey: Prentice-Hall.

Sellers, Martha G. (1969) "Transracial Adoption," Child Welfare, 48, June.

Shaw, Lulie A. (1953) "Following up Adoptions," British Journal of Psychiatric Social Work, November.

Sheperd, Elizabeth (1964) "Adopting Negro Children ," The New Republic, June.

Siegel, Sidney (1956) Nonparametric Statistics for the Behavioral Sciences, New York: McGraw-Hill.

Social Planning Council of Metropolitan Toronto (1966) The Adoption of Negro Children: A Community-Wide Approach , Toronto: Social Planning Council.

St. Denis, Gerald C. (1969) "Interracial Adoptions in Minnesota: Self Concept and Child Rearing Attitudes of Caucasian Parents Who Have Adopted Negro Children," Doctoral dissertation, University of Minnesota, Minneapolis.

Terman, L. M. (1938) Psychological Factors in Marital Happiness, New York: McGraw-Hill.

Theis, Sophie V. S. (1924) How Foster Children Turn Out, New York State Charities Aid Association.

Thompson, Daniel (1966) "The Formation of Social Attitudes," in _Racial and Ethnic Relations_, Bernard E. Segal (ed.), New York: Crowell.

Toussieng, P. (1962) "Thoughts Regarding the Etiology of Psychological Differences in Adopted Children," _Child Welfare_, 41, February.

Valk, Margaret (1957) _Korean-American Children in American Adoptive Homes_, New York: Child Welfare League of America, September.

Warner, L. Lloyd & Srole, Leo (1945) _The Social Systems of American Ethnic Groups_, New Haven: Yale University Press.

Witmer, Helen, et al. (1963) _Independent Adoptions_, New York: Russell Sage Foundation.

Wittenborn, Richard J. (1957) The Placement of Adoptive Children, Springfield, Illinois: Charles C. Thomas.

Woods, Sister Francis J. & Lancaster, Alice C. (1962) "Cultural Factors in Negro Adoptive Parenthood," _Social Work_, October.

SAMPLE LETTER USED BY AGENCIES AS A GUIDE IN COMPOSING LETTER TO
TRANSRACIAL ADOPTIVE PARENTS; THE LETTER ASKED IF THE PARENTS
WERE INTERESTED IN PARTICIPATING IN THE PROJECT

(Sample Letter to Adoptive Parents of a Black Child)

Date

Mr. & Mrs. _____
_____, Street
_____, Wisconsin

Dear Mr. and Mrs. _____:

The School of Social Work at the University of Wisconsin, in cooperation with the adoption agencies in Wisconsin is conducting a study to learn more about the experiences of couples who have adopted a Black (or part-Black) child. At present there is little information available about what couples who have adopted a Black child think about their experience.

Our agency is cooperating in this study, and we believe the results will be of value in improving services to other Black children in need of adoptive homes. We are writing to ask if you would be willing to share your thoughts about the experiences you have had with an interviewer who would come to your home?

The interviewer is associated with the University of Wisconsin, and is not a member of our staff. The interview would be confidential and your name would not appear in any report. In addition to yourselves, more than 50 other couples throughout Wisconsin who have adopted a Black child are being asked if they are willing to participate. The interviewer is not concerned with seeing or talking to your children, but only with meeting with both of you.

Your participation in this study is voluntary, and we will understand if you feel you cannot participate. Whatever your decision, please fill out the enclosed reply card and return it to our agency.

If you agree to participate, the Judge of the County where your child was adopted will be asked to give his permission for an interviewer to meet with you. If the Judge's consent is obtained, an interviewer will contact you (perhaps 5 or 6 weeks from now) to arrange a mutually convenient time for an interview.

If you have questions about this study, please call.

Sincerely yours,

(Agency) Director

Appendix B

SAMPLE LETTER USED BY AGENCILS AS A GUIDE IN COMPOSING LETTER TO
INTRARACIAL ADOPTIVE PARENTS; THE LETTER ASKED IF THE PARENTS
WERE INTERESTED IN PARTICIPATING IN THE PROJECT

(Sample Letter to Adoptive Parents of a White Child)

Date

Mr. & Mrs. _____
_____, Street
_____, Wisconsin

Dear Mr. and Mrs. _____:

The School of Social Work at the University of Wisconsin, in cooperation with adoption agencies in Wisconsin is conducting a study to learn more about the experiences of couples who have adopted a child.

Our agency is cooperating in this study, and we believe the results will be of value in improving services to other children in need of adoptive homes. We are writing to ask if you would be willing to share your thoughts about the experiences you have had with an interviewer who would come to your home.

The interviewer is associated with the University of Wisconsin, and is not a member of our staff. The interview would be confidential, and your name would not appear in any report. In addition to yourselves, more than 100 couples throughout Wisconsin who have adopted a child are being asked if they are willing to participate. The interviewer is not concerned with seeing or talking to your children, but only with meeting with both of you.

Your participation in this study is voluntary, and we will understand if you feel you cannot participate. Whatever your decision, please fill out the enclosed reply card and return it to our agency.

If you agree to participate, the Judge of the County where your child was adopted will be asked to give his permission for an interviewer to meet with you. If the Judge's consent is obtained, an interviewer will contact you (perhaps 4 or 5 weeks from now) to arrange a mutually convenient time for an interview.

If you have questions about this study, please call.

Sincerely yours,

(Agency) Director

Appendix C

RETURN POSTAL CARD FOR ADOPTIVE PARENTS TO INDICATE IF WILLING TO BE INTERVIEWED

We are (check one)

_____ willing _____ not willing

to talk to an interviewer.

Mr. & Mrs. _____

        (Father's first name)   (Last name)

If you check "willing," please indicate your address:

_____

Street or Rural Route

_____

City   State

Appendix D

WARNER, MEEKER, EELS'S REVISED SCALE FOR RATING OCCUPATION, AS PRESENTED IN HANDBOOK OF RESEARCH DESIGN AND SOCIAL MEASUREMENT BY DELBERT C. MILLER, NEW YORK: DAVID McKAY, 1964

Rating Assigned to Occupation	Professionals	Proprietors and Managers	Business Men	Clerks and Kindred Workers, Etc.	Manual Workers	Protective and Service Workers	Farmers
1	Lawyers, doctors, dentists, engineers, judges, high-school superintendents, veterinarians, ministers (graduated from divinity school), chemists, etc., with postgraduate training, architects	Businesses valued at $75,000 and over	Regional and divisional managers of large financial and industrial enterprises	Certified Public Accountants			Gentlemen farmers
2	High-school teachers, trained nurses, chiropractors, undertakers, ministers (some training), newspaper editors, librarians (graduate)	Businesses valued at $20,000 to $75,000	Assistant managers and office and department managers of large businesses, assistants to executives, etc.	Accountants, salesmen of real estate and insurance, postmasters			Large farm owners, farm owners

97

Rating Assigned to Occupation	Professionals	Proprietors and Managers	Business Men	Clerks and Kindred Workers, Etc.	Manual Workers	Protective and Service Workers	Farmers
3	Social workers, grade-school teachers, optometrists, librarians (not graduate), undertaker's assistants, ministers (no training)	Businesses valued at $5,000 to $20,000	All minor officials of businesses	Auto salesmen, bank clerks and cashiers, postal clerks, secretaries to executives, supervisors of railroad, telephone, etc., justices of the peace	Contractors		
4		Businesses valued at $2,000 to $5,000		Stenographers,	Factory foreman, electricians, plumbers, carpenters, watchmakers (own business)	Dry cleaners, butchers, sheriffs, railroad engineers and conductors	
5		Businesses valued at $500 to $2,000		Dime store clerks, hardware salesmen, beauty operators, telephone operators	Carpenters, plumbers, electricians (apprentice), timekeepers, linemen, telephone or telegraph, radio repairmen, medium skilled workers	Barbers, firemen, butcher's apprentices, practical nurses, policemen, seamstresses, cooks in restaurant, bartenders	Tenant farmers

Rating Assigned to Occupation	Professionals	Proprietors and Managers	Business Men	Clerks and Kindred Workers, Etc.	Manual Workers	Protective and Service Workers	Farmers
6		Business valued at less than $500			Moulders, semi-skilled workers, assistants to carpenter, etc.	Baggagemen, night policemen, taxi and truck drivers, gas station attendants, waitresses in restaurants	Small tenant farmers, laborers
7					Heavy labor, migrant work, odd-job men, miners	Janitors, scrubwomen, newsboys	Migrant farm laborers

LETTER TO COUNTY JUDGES REQUESTING LEGAL PERMISSION TO
INCLUDE TRANSRACIAL ADOPTIVE FAMILIES IN STUDY

STATE OF WISCONSIN/Department of Health & Social Services

Division of Family Services
1 West Wilson Street
Madison, Wisconsin 53702

Honorable

Dear Judge

A doctoral candidate (Charles Zastrow) in the School of Social work at the University of Wisconsin has developed for his dissertation a study to obtain, through interviews with adoptive parents , a better picture of the satisfactions derived and difficulties encountered by white couples who have adopted a Black child.

Two groups of subjects compose the study group; a group of 50 white parents who adopted a Black child, and a group of 50 white couples who adopted a child of their own race. The latter group is being included in order to compare similarities and differences in satisfactions derived and difficulties encountered between inter-racially and intra-racially adopting parents.

The study has been reviewed and approved by Mr. Zastrow's doctoral committee; the chairman of which is Dr. Alfred Kadushin, a nationally recognized authority in the child welfare field. A few years ago, Dr. Kadushin conducted a study in Wisconsin on school-age children placed for adoption that had a similar design.

Our Division has examined and approved the study, and is assiting in identifying the study group. We believe the results will be useful in improving services to other Black children who are available for adoption.

The following procedures are being followed in selecting the study group. Adoption agencies in the State first identified adoptive families meeting the criteria for the study group. The agencies then sent a letter to these parents explaining the nature and sponsorship of the project, and asking if they would be willing to share their thoughts about their adoptive experiences with an interviewer. The names of the adoptive couples willing to participate were then mailed to our office.

Attached to this letter are the names of the couples indicating a willingness to participate whose adoptions were completed in your county.

We request your permission to provide the names of these couples to the project staff; and permission for the project staff to interview these parents and to have access to the adoption record material. Mr. Zastrow (project director at the School of Social Work) has assured us the interviews will be confidential and that the names of the families will not appear in any report.

Your response to this request may be facilitated by filling out the enclosed reply card.

If there are questions about the project, please call either Miss Verna Lauritzen (266-255) who has been the staff person most involved in the project at our office, or Mr. Zastrow (257-4737).

Sincerely,

Frank Newgent, Administrator
DIVISION OF FAMILY SERVICES

Appendix F

LETTER TO COUNTY JUDGES REQUESTING LEGAL PERMISSION TO
INCLUDE INTRARACIAL ADOPTIVE FAMILIES IN STUDY

STATE OF WISCONSIN/Department of Health & Social Services

Division of Family Services
1 West Wilson Street
Madison, Wisconsin 53702

Honorable

Dear Judge

Several weeks ago we requested and received your permission to include in an Adoption Study selected parents who had adopted a Black child in your county. These families had previously indicated in response to a letter from the agency through which they adopted a child that they were willing to be interviewed about their adoptive experiences.

As you may recall from our prior letter, the study was designed at the School of Social Work (University of Wisconsin), and our Division and adoption agencies in the State are assisting in identifying the study group. The general purpose of the study is to obtain, through interviews with adoptive parents, a better picture of the satisfactions derived and difficulties encountered by white couples who have adopted a Black child. Two groups of subjects compose the study group; a group of 50 white couples who adopted a Black child, and a group of 50 white couples who adopted a child of their own race. The latter group is being included in order to compare the experiences of inter-racial adoptive parents to the experiences of intra-racial adoptive parents.

The design of the study required that the inter-racial adoptive families be selected first, and then for the intra-racial adoptive families to be selected and matched on certain characteristics to the inter-racial group. Permission from county judges to include the inter-racial group in the study was received some time ago, and the interviewing of this group is nearly completed; with initial results indicating the worthwhileness of the project.

The selection of the intra-racial adoptive families has now been completed. At the end of this letter are the names of the couples indicating a willingness to participate whose adoptions were completed in your county.

The families' willingness to participate was obtained by the following procedures. Agencies sent a letter to these families explaining the nature and sponsorship of the project, and asking if they would be willing to share their thoughts about their adoptive experiences with an interviewer. The names of the adoptive couples willing to participate were then mailed to our office.

We request your permission to provide the names of these couples to the project staff; and permission for the project staff to interview these parents and to have access to the adoption record material. Mr. Zastrow (project director at the School of Social Work) has assured us the interviews will be confidential and that the names of the families will not appear in any report.

Your response to this request may be facilitated by filling out the enclosed reply card.

If there are questions about the project, please call either Miss Verna Lauritzen (266-2555) who has been the staff person most involved in the project at our office, or Mr. Zastrow (257-4737).

Sincerely,

Frank Newgent, Administrator
DIVISION OF FAMILY SERVICES

RETURN POSTAL CARD FOR COUNTY JUDGES TO INDICATE IF REQUESTED LEGAL
PERMISSION FOR INCLUDING ADOPTIVE FAMILIES IN STUDY IS GRANTED

The requested permission in your _____ , 1970

                                            (mo.)   (day)

letter for the families indicated is:

_____ granted   _____ not granted

                                  _____

                                  (Judge's Signature)

Appendix H

LETTER TO STUDY GROUP PARENTS EXPRESSING APPRECIATION FOR THEIR
WILLINGNESS TO PARTICIPATE, AND INDICATING AN INTERVIEWER
WILL SOON TELEPHONE TO ARRANGE A CONVENIENT TIME FOR AN INTERVIEW

(This particular copy was sent to the families who
were interviewed by the Wisconsin Survey
Research Lab interviewers.)

School of Social Work
University of Wisconsin
100 Observatory Hill Drive
Madison, Wisconsin 53706

A few months ago you indicated in response to a letter from the agency through which you adopted a child that you are willing to participate in an adoption study by discussing your adoptive experiences with an interviewer. The study was designed at the School of Social Work, and is being conducted with the cooperation of adoption agencies in the State.

We wish to express our appreciation for your willingness to participate. Permission for an interviewer to meet with you was recently granted by the Judge of the County where you adopted your child.

An interviewer from the Survey Research Laboratory at the University of Wisconsin will be calling you within the next few weeks to arrange a mutually convenient time for an interview. Let me assure you that the interview will be confidential. This is a statistical study and no names will be used in any report.

The interviewer is not concerned with seeing or talking to your children, but only with meeting with both of you. Since the interview will focus on your personal experiences, you may wish to arrange to have the interview in a place in your home where it will be relatively private.

Thank you once again for your willingness to participate in this study.

Sincerely,

Charles H. Zastrow
Ph.D. Candidate

CHZ/kmz

INTERVIEW SCHEDULE FOR TRANSRACIAL ADOPTIVE PARENTS

Interview Schedule

We want to know what it is like to be adoptive parents, and believe the best way to find out is to talk with parents like yourselves who have adopted a child. Nobody knows as well as you what it is like to be adoptive parents.

Whatever you tell us will be considered confidential. No names will ever be revealed.

In responding to the questions we will be asking, we want you to think primarily in terms of _____ (NAME OF CHILD). When we are referring to _____'s (CHILD) race, may we use the term Negro, or would you prefer to use some other term?

                    Other term: _____

1. We'll start by asking how many children you now have living here, including _____ (CHILD)?   Number _____

2. Will you give me the name, sex and age of each (this) child?

        Name   Sex   Age

    _____   _____   _____
    _____   _____   _____
    _____   _____   _____
    _____   _____   _____
    _____   _____   _____
    _____   _____   _____

3. Thinking of the time prior to your adopting _____ (CHILD), can you tell me the reasons why you were considering adopting?

    _____
    _____
    _____
    _____
    _____

Interviewer's Name: _____   Int. No.: _____

Date: _____   Time Started: _____

4. At that time did you have a preference for a girl or for a boy?

_____ Girl   _____ Boy   _____ No preference
         ↓   ↓   (TO Q 5)

(If Preference Noted)   What were your reasons for wanting a girl (boy)?

_____
_____
_____
_____

5. Did you prefer a Negro child when you <u>first</u> considered this adoption?

_____ Yes   _____ No
(TO Q 6)   ↓

5a. Did someone suggest that you adopt a Negro child?

_____ Yes   _____ No
         ↓   (TO Q 6)

Who was this: _____
               _____

6. At that time did you consider adopting a child of some other race besides Negro or white?

_____ Yes   _____ No
         ↓   ↓

6a. What other races did   6d. Were there any special reasons
     you consider?   why you did not consider a child
                                        of some other race?

_____   _____
_____   _____
_____   _____
                                       _____
          ↓   _____
                                       _____
6b. Were there any special   _____
     reasons why you did not
     adopt a child of this race
     (these races)?

_____
_____
_____
_____
_____

7. What were your reasons for deciding to adopt a Negro child?

   _____
   _____
   _____
   _____
   _____

8. What reservations did you have at the time when you were considering
   adopting _____ (CHILD)?

   _____
   _____
   _____
   _____

9. I'd like you to think back to the day when you first saw _____
   (CHILD) in person. What were your reactions on seeing him/her for the
   first time?

   _____
   _____
   _____
   _____
   _____

10. Being a parent brings certain satisfactions. What has been the one
    most satisfying thing to you in having _____ (CHILD) in your home
    as your child?

                   Mother   Father

    _____   _____
    _____   _____
    _____   _____
    _____   _____
    _____   _____

11. What else have you found satisfying about having _____ (CHILD) in
    your home?

   _____
   _____
   _____
   _____

12. What do you see as _____'s (CHILD) special strengths? His/her
    good points?

   _____
   _____
   _____
   _____
   _____

13. What has _____ (CHILD) added to your lives?

_____
_____
_____
_____
_____

14. As every parent knows, being a parent not only has satisfactions, but also some dissatisfactions. What has been the one most dissatisfying thing to you in having _____ (CHILD) in your home as your child?

        Mother   Father

_____   _____
_____   _____
_____   _____
_____   _____
_____   _____

15. What else have you found dissatisfying about having _____ (CHILD) in your home?

_____
_____
_____
_____
_____

16. As any parent knows, all children have some faults, some shortcomings. What are _____'s (CHILD) shortcomings?

_____
_____
_____
_____
_____

17. We have been talking about some of the satisfactions and dissatisfactions that you have experienced in having _____ (CHILD) in your family. In this study we are also interested in finding out how relatives, friends and neighbors of adoptive parents have reacted to the adoption. Can you tell me what were the reactions of your relatives when they first heard you were going to adopt _____ (CHILD):

        FIRST HEARD   17a. How do these people feel about _____ (CHILD) now?

_____   _____
_____   _____
_____   _____
_____   _____
_____   _____

18. What were the reactions of your friends and neighbors when they first heard you were going to adopt _____ (CHILD)?

FIRST HEARD

18a. How do these people feel about _____ (CHILD) now?

_____   _____
_____   _____
_____   _____
_____   _____

19. (IF THE PARENTS HAVE OTHER CHILDREN) How did your other children react to _____ (CHILD) when they first saw him/her?

_____
_____
_____
_____
_____

19a. How do they feel about _____ (CHILD) now?

_____
_____
_____
_____
_____

20. What have been the reactions of strangers when they discovered _____ (CHILD) is a member of your family?

_____
_____
_____
_____

(Ask questions 21 thru 23 if child is 3 years of age or over; if under 3 go to question 24).

21. Is _____ (CHILD) aware he/she is adopted?

_____ Yes   _____ No
                                      (TO Q 22)

21a. How did he/she react on becoming aware of this?

_____
_____
_____
_____
_____

22. Has _____ (CHILD) asked questions about the color of his/her skin?

_____ Yes   _____ No
        ↓   (TO Q 23)

22a. How have you dealt with such questions?

_____
_____
_____
_____

23. Is _____ (CHILD) aware of his/her Negro ancestry?

_____ Yes   _____ No
        ↓   (TO Q 24)

23a. What has been his/her reactions to being Negro?

_____
_____
_____
_____

24. How does _____ (CHILD) get along with other children in the neighborhood?

_____
_____
_____
_____

25. Has he/she been teased or called names by neighborhood children because of the color of his/her skin?

_____ Yes   _____ No   _____ Do not know
       ↓   (TO Q 26)   (TO Q 26)

25a. What has been _____'s (CHILD) reaction?

_____
_____

25b. How have you dealt with such comments?

_____
_____
_____

26. We all have certain difficulties as we go through life, but do you expect _____ (CHILD) to have any particular problems because of his/her race when he/she enters grammar school?

_____ Yes   _____ No

26a. What?   26b. Is there a special reason you feel this way

_____   _____
_____   _____
_____   _____
_____   _____
_____   _____
_____   _____

27. (Ask this question if child is 4 years of age or older; if under 4 to to question 28) Is _____ (CHILD) attending either nursery school or kindergarten?

_____ Yes   _____ No
                                          (TO Q 28)

27a. Has _____ (CHILD) encountered any difficulties because of race in this school?

_____ Yes   _____ No
                                          (TO Q 28)

27b. What?

_____
_____
_____
_____

28. Do you expect any specific difficulties because of race when he/she seeks employment?

_____ Yes   _____ No

28a. What?   28b. Is there a special reason you feel this way?

_____   _____
_____   _____
_____   _____
_____   _____
_____   _____
_____   _____

112

29. Do you expect specific problems because of race when he/she begins to date?

_____ Yes   _____ No

29a. What?   29b. Any special reason?

_____   _____
_____   _____
_____   _____
_____   _____
_____   _____

30. Looking back on your experience with _____ (CHILD), in what ways, if any, is it different from what you anticipated, expected, or pictured it to be?

_____
_____
_____
_____
_____

31. In what ways, if any, do you think this child is "right" for you; that is, well-matched to you?

_____
_____
_____
_____
_____

32. In what ways, if any, do you think _____ (CHILD) is not "well-matched" to you?

_____
_____
_____
_____
_____

33. Do you feel, now, that _____ (CHILD) is really your own child?

| _____ Yes | _____ No | _____ Depends |
| ↓ | ↓ | ↓ |

33a. How long after _____
(CHILD) was placed with
you did it take before
you felt he/she was
really your own?

Number of months _____

↓

33b. (IF LONGER THAN 2 MONTHS)
Why do you think it took
this length of time?

33c. Why not?

33d. On what does it
depend?

_____
_____
_____

34. Besides the obvious differences, in what ways to you think adoptive
parenthood is different from biological parenthood?

_____
_____
_____
_____
_____

35. Have there been times when you were especially glad that you had
adopted a Negro child?

| _____ Yes | _____ No |
| ↓ | (TO Q 36) |

35a. What were the circumstances associated with this?

_____
_____
_____
_____
_____

36. What do you think are the special satisfactions obtained by White
adoptive parents of a Negro child?

_____
_____
_____
_____
_____

37. As you know, all families have their problems, some a little more
    serious, some less serious. Were there times, when you felt you had
    made a mistake by adopting a <u>Negro</u> child?

    _____ Yes   _____ No
           ↓   (TO Q 38)

    37a. What were the circumstances associated with this?

    _____
    _____
    _____
    _____
    _____

38. What special problems do you think White adoptive parents of a <u>Negro</u>
    child face?

    _____
    _____
    _____
    _____
    _____

39. What special qualities do you think are required in being a White
    adoptive parent for a Negro child?

    _____
    _____
    _____
    _____
    _____

40. What types of people, if any, do you think should <u>not</u> adopt a <u>Negro</u>
    child?

    _____
    _____
    _____
    _____
    _____

41. What special problems do you think a Negro child adopted by White
    parents will have in establishing a self-identity?

    _____
    _____
    _____
    _____

42. If you had a close friend who was seriously considering adopting a Negro child, what would you tell this friend?

_____
_____
_____
_____
_____

43. Looking back on your adoptive experience, if you knew at the beginning, what you know now, would you still adopt a Negro child?

_____ Yes   _____ No   _____ Depends
(TO Q 44)   ↓   ↓

43a. Why not: 43b. What would it
                                      depend on?

_____   _____
_____   _____
_____   _____
_____   _____
_____   _____

44. One of the reasons for doing this study is to obtain suggestions for ways in which adoptive agencies can improve their services to couples who are in the process of adopting a Negro child. What do you think your agency might have done differently to help make your experience as adoptive parents more successful and satisfying.

_____
_____
_____
_____

45. I have only two more questions to ask.
Would you be interested in periodically getting together with other couples who have adopted a child of another race in order to share and discuss you experiences and concerns?

_____ Yes   _____ No   _____ Uncertain

46. Are you presently a member, or have you thought about joining the Open Door Society?

_____ Member
_____ Nonmember, interested in joining
_____ Nonmember, not interested in joining
_____ Have not heard of Open Door Society

INTERVIEWER NOTE: If parents ask what an Open Door Society is, indicate "an Open Door Society is a group made up of couples who have adopted a child of another race that meet to share and discuss their experiences and concerns."

116

That concludes the questions I have. However, before ending this interview, I would like each of you to fill out a brief, 2-page form that has questions relating to your adoptive experience. When filling out this form, please do not discuss your answers with one another.

Note: Just before giving a form to each parent, check the appropriate blank on the second page for "Mother" or "Father" indicating the person who will fill out the form--then give a form to each parent.

This is not a test, and there are no right or wrong answers. Your thoughts about each question are "Right" for you, and you should answer that way. Please be sure to answer every question.

INTERVIEWER'S RATING OF OVERALL PARENTAL SATISFACTIONS

While the parents are filling out the questionnaire, check (for each parent) the phrase on the following scale which best expresses your impression of how satis-fying each parent feels his/her adoptive experience with _____ (CHILD) has been:

MOTHER

_____ Extremely satisfying

_____ More satisfying than dis-satisfying

_____ About half and half

_____ More dissatisfying than satisfying

_____ Extremely dissatisfying

FATHER

_____ Extremely satisfying

_____ More satisfying than dis-satisfying

_____ About half and half

_____ More dissatisfying than satisfying

_____ Extremely dissatisfying

INTERVIEWER'S SUPPLEMENT

A1. Write your name and the interview number on both questionnaires.

A2. Make sure you completely fill in all data requested on the Cover Sheet.

A3. Time interview ended: _____

117

A4. Other persons present at interview besides the adoptive parents were:

_____ None   _____ Other children

_____ Adopted child   _____ Other adults

_____ Own children other than
        adopted child

THUMBNAIL SKETCH

_____

_____

_____

_____

_____

_____

_____

_____

_____

_____

_____

Appendix J

INTERVIEW SCHEDULE FOR INTRARACIAL ADOPTIVE PARENTS

Interview Schedule

We want to know what it is like to be adoptive parents, and believe the best way to find out is to talk with parents like yourselves who have adopted a child. Nobody knows as well as you what it is like to be adoptive parents.

Whatever you tell us will be considered confidential. No names will ever be revealed.

In responding to the questions we will be asking, we want you to think primarily in terms of _____ (NAME OF CHILD).

1. We'll start by asking how many children you now have living here, including _____ (CHILD)?   Number _____

2. Will you give me the name, sex and age of each (this) child?

Name	Sex	Age

3. Thinking of the time prior to your adopting _____ (CHILD), can you tell me the reasons why you were considering adopting?

_____

_____

_____

_____

_____

Interviewer's Name: _____   Int. No.: _____

Date: _____   Time Started: _____

119

4. At that time did you have a preference for a girl or for a boy?

    _____ Girl   _____ Boy   _____ No preference
           ↓   ↓

    (If Preference Noted) What were your reasons for wanting a girl (boy)?

    _____
    _____
    _____
    _____

5. At that time did you consider adopting a child of some other race besides white?

    _____ Yes   _____ No
           ↓   ↓

    5a. What other races did you   5c. Were there any special reasons
         consider?   why you did not consider a
                                            child of some other race?

         _____   _____
                                            _____
                                            _____
    5b. Were there any special reasons   _____
         why you did not adopt a child   _____
         of this race (these races)?   _____

         _____
         _____
         _____
         _____
         _____

6. What reservations did you have at the time when you were considering
    adopting _____ (CHILD)?

    _____
    _____
    _____
    _____
    _____

7. I'd like you to think back to the day when you first saw _____ (CHILD)
    in person. What were your reactions on seeing him/her for the first time?

    _____
    _____
    _____
    _____

8. Being a parent brings certain satisfactions. What has been the one most satisfying thing to you in having _____ (CHILD) in your home as your child?

MOTHER   FATHER

_____   _____
_____   _____
_____   _____
_____   _____
_____   _____

9. What else have you found satisfying about having _____ (CHILD) in your home?

_____
_____
_____
_____
_____

10. What do you see as _____'s (CHILD) special strengths? His/her good points?

_____
_____
_____
_____
_____

11. What has _____ (CHILD) added to your lives?

_____
_____
_____
_____

12. As every parent knows, being a parent not only has satisfactions, but also some dissatisfactions. What has been the one most dissatisfying thing to you in having _____ (CHILD) in your home as your child?

_____   _____
_____   _____
_____   _____
_____   _____

13. What else have you found dissatisfying about having _____ (CHILD) in your home?

_____
_____
_____
_____

14. As any parent knows, all children have some faults, some shortcomings. What are _____'s (CHILD) shortcomings?

_____
_____
_____
_____
_____

15. We have been talking about some of the satisfactions and dissatisfactions that you have experienced in having _____ (CHILD) in your family. In this study we are also interested in finding out how relatives, friends and neighbors of adoptive parents have reacted to the adoption. Can you tell me what were the reactions of your relatives when they first heard you were going to adopt _____ (CHILD)?

      FIRST HEARD

15a. How do these people feel about _____ (CHILD) now?

16. What were the reactions of your friends and neighbors when they first heard you were going to adopt _____ (CHILD)?

      FIRST HEARD

16a. How do these people feel about _____ (CHILD) now?

17. (IF THE PARENTS HAVE OTHER CHILDREN) How did your other children react to _____ (CHILD) when they first saw him/her?

_____
_____
_____
_____
_____

18. (ASK THIS QUESTION IF CHILD IS THREE YEARS OF AGE OR OVER; IF UNDER THREE GO
     TO QUESTION 19)   Is _____ (CHILD) aware he/she is adopted?

     _____ Yes   _____ No
            ↓   (TO Q 19)

     18a. How did he/she react on becoming aware of this?

     _____
     _____
     _____
     _____
     _____

19. How does _____ (CHILD) get along with other children in the neighbor-
     hood?

     _____
     _____
     _____
     _____
     _____

20. Looking back on your adoptive experience with _____ (CHILD), in what
     ways, if any, is it different from what you anticipated, expected, or pic-
     tured it to be?

     _____
     _____
     _____
     _____
     _____

21. In what ways, if any, do you think this child is "right" for you; that is,
     well-matched to you?

     _____
     _____
     _____
     _____
     _____

22. In what ways, if any, do you think _____ (CHILD) is not "well-matched"
     to you?

     _____
     _____
     _____
     _____
     _____

23. Do you feel, now, that _____ (CHILD) is really your own child?

_____ Yes   _____ No   _____ Depends

      ↓   ↓   ↓

    23a. How long after _____   23c. Why not?   23d. On what does
         (CHILD) was placed with   it depend?
         you did it take before
         you felt he/she was   _____   _____
         really your own?   _____   _____

         Number of months _____   _____   _____
                                         _____   _____
                                         _____   _____
            ↓   _____   _____

    23b. (IF LONGER THAN 2 MONTHS)
         Why do you think it took
         this length of time?

         _____
         _____
         _____

24. Besides the obvious differences, in what ways do you think adoptive
parenthood is different from biological parenthood?

_____
_____
_____
_____
_____

25. Have there been times when you were especially glad that you had adopted a
child?

_____ Yes   _____ No
      ↓   (TO Q 26)

25a. What were the circumstances associated with this?

_____
_____
_____
_____
_____

26. As you know, all families have their problems, some a little more serious, some less serious. Were there times when you felt you had made a mistake by adopting a child?

_____ Yes   _____ No
         ↓   (TO Q 27)

26a. What were the circumstances associated with this?

_____
_____
_____
_____
_____

27. What special problems do you think adoptive parents face?

_____
_____
_____
_____
_____

28. What special qualities do you think are required in being an adoptive parent?

_____
_____
_____
_____
_____

29. What types of people, if any, do you think should not adopt a child?

_____
_____
_____
_____
_____

30. If you had a close friend who was seriously considering adopting a child, what would you tell this friend?

_____
_____
_____
_____

31. Looking back on your adoptive experience, if you knew at the beginning, what you know now, would you still adopt a child?

_____ Yes   _____ No   _____ Depends

                         ↓   ↓

              31a. Why not   31b. What would it depend on?

              _____   _____
              _____   _____
              _____   _____
              _____   _____
              _____   _____

32. One of the reasons for doing this study is to obtain suggestions for ways in which adoptive agencies can improve their services to couples who are in the process of adopting. What do you think your agency might have done differently to help make your experience as adoptive parents more success-ful and satisfying?

    _____
    _____
    _____
    _____
    _____
    _____

    That concludes the questions I have. However, before ending this interview, I would like each of you to fill out a brief, 2-page form that has questions related to your adoptive experience. When filling out this form, please do not discuss your answers with one another.

    NOTE: JUST BEFORE GIVING THE FORM TO EACH PARENT, CHECK THE APPROPRIATE BLANK ON THE SECOND PAGE FOR "MOTHER" OR "FATHER" INDICATING THE PERSON WHO WILL FILL OUT THE FORM--THEN GIVE A FORM TO EACH PARENT.

    This is not a test, and there are no right or wrong answers. Your thoughts about each question are "Right" for you, and you should answer that way. Please be sure to answer every question.

INTERVIEWER'S RATING OF OVERALL PARENTAL SATISFACTIONS

    While the parents are filling out the questionnaire, check (for each parent) the phrase on the following scale which best expresses your impression of how satisfying each parent feels his/her adoptive experience with _____ (CHILD) has been:

MOTHER	FATHER
_____ Extremely satisfying	_____ Extremely satisfying
_____ More satisfying than dissatisfying	_____ More satisfying than dissatisfying
_____ About half and half	_____ About half and half
_____ More dissatisfying than satisfying	_____ More dissatisfying than satisfying
_____ Extremely dissatisfying	_____ Extremely dissatisfying

INTERVIEWER'S SUPPLEMENT

A1. Write your name and the interview number on both questionnaires.

A2. Make sure you completely fill in all data requested on the Cover sheet.

A3. Time interview ended: _____

A4. Other persons present at interview besides the adoptive parents were:

_____ None   _____ Other children

_____ Adopted child   _____ Other adults

_____ Own children other
        than adopted child

THUMBNAIL SKETCH

_____
_____
_____
_____
_____
_____
_____
_____
_____
_____
_____
_____

Appendix K

ADOPTION RECORD SCHEDULE

THE CHILD

Name:

    Child: _____
          (Adoptive Name)

    Adoptive parents: _____

    Adoptive agency : _____

I.   Background Information

    1.   Sex: Male _____   Female _____

    2.   Birthdate: _____

    3.   Race: % Negro _____   % White _____   % Other _____
                                                 (Specify) _____

    4.   Religion (before adopted)
        a) Catholic ____   c) Jewish ____
        b) Protestant ____ d) Other (specify) ____   e) Unaffiliated ____

    5.   Age at time of separation from natural parents: years ____ months ____

    6.   Length of time between separation from natural parents and placement with adoptive parents: years ____ months ____

    7.   Number of placements following separation from natural parents before being placed with adoptive parents: _____

    8.   Date placed with adoptive family: _____

II.   Behavioral problems mentioned in record prior to adoptive placement

    _____1. Feeding difficulties--picky eater, food fads, overeats

    _____2. Sleeping difficulties--nightmares, sleepwalking

    _____3. Nervous tics, nervous habits

    _____4. Neurotic fears

    _____5. Enuresis

    _____6. Masturbation--sexplay

    _____7. Hyperactivity

_____8. Temper tantrums

_____9. Destructive behavior

_____10. Nail biting, thumb sucking

_____11. Sibling rivalry

_____12. Shy , withdrawn, daydreams

_____13. Disobedient ·

_____14. Learning difficulties

_____15. Affectionateless, aloof

_____16. Overdemanding for attention

_____17. Speech difficulty

_____18. Over-reacts , cries easily

_____19. Other (specify)

_____
_____
_____
_____
_____
_____

III.   Total number of behavior problems mentioned in record prior to adoptive placement: _____

IV.   Serious physical and medical handicaps and problems mentioned in record prior to adoptive placement (specify):

1. _____

2. _____

3. _____

4. _____

5. _____

ADOPTIVE FAMILY

I.   Identifying Data

Names

        Adoptive Father _____

        Adoptive Mother _____

        Adoptive Child _____

Address _____
            (street)   (city, town, village)   (state)

Adoptive Agency _____

II.   Background Data

    1. Age at time of placement

    2. Occupation

    3. Education (last grade completed)

    4. Birthdate

    5. Number of years married at time of
        adoptive placement

    6. Composition of family at time of
        adoptive placement:

	Initials	Age	Sex
Own children	_____	_____	_____
	_____	_____	_____
	_____	_____	_____
	_____	_____	_____
	_____	_____	_____
	_____	_____	_____
Adopted children	_____	_____	_____
	_____	_____	_____
Foster children	_____	_____	_____
	_____	_____	_____
Relatives (specify rela-tionship to adopted child)	_____	_____	_____

7. Religious affiliations   Mother   Father

    a) Catholic
                                                      _____   _____
    b) Protestant
                                                      _____   _____
    c) Jewish
                                                      _____   _____
    d) Other (specify) _____
                                                      _____   _____
    e) No affiliation
                                                      _____   _____

III. Adoption History of Parents

    1) Applied for child previously: ____ Yes ____ No ____ Information
        (If Yes)   unavailable
        a. Applied at this or some other agency ____ Yes ____ No
        b. Received a child   ____ Yes ____ No
        c. If did not receive a child, what were
            the reasons? _____
            _____
            _____
            _____

        d. Applied through Independent Sources   ____ Yes   ____ No

                                                   ____ Information
                                                        unavailable
        e. Received a child   ____ Yes   ____ No
        f. If did not receive a child, what were
            the reasons? _____
            _____
            _____
            _____

    2) When applied to agency this time, requested a white child
                          ____ Yes   ____ No
        (For Parents Who Applied For a White Child, But Adopted a Black Child)
        Reasons parents did not receive a white child:

            _____
            _____
            _____
            _____

    3) (For Inter-Racial Adoptive Parents) Who initiated discussion of the
        possibility of adopting a Black child?

            _____1. Worker

            _____2. Adoptive father

            _____3. Adoptive mother

            _____4. Adoptive couples

131

_____ 5. Statement on application form

_____ 6. Information not available

4) (For Parents Adopting a White Child) Parents considered adopting a child of some other rate besides white?

____ Yes   ____ Information   ____ No
                     Unavailable

What other races were   Reasons for not considering
considered?   a child of some other race:

_____   _____
_____   _____
_____   _____
_____   _____

Reasons why a child of one of
these races was not adopted:

_____
_____
_____
_____

5) (For Parents Adopting a Black Child) Parents considered adopting a child of some other race besides Black or white?

____ Yes   ____ Information   ____ No
                     Unavailable

What other races were   Reasons for not considering
considered?   a child of some other race?

_____   _____
_____   _____
_____   _____
_____   _____

Reasons why a child of one of
these races was not adopted?

_____
_____
_____
_____

6) Parents considered adopting either a handicapped or an older child:

____ Yes   ____ Information   ____ No
                     unavailable

Types of these hard-to-   Reasons why such a child was
place children considered: not considered:

_____   _____
_____   _____
_____   _____
_____   _____

Reasons why one of these
children was not adopted:

_____
_____
_____
_____

IV.   Capability for natural parenthood at time of placement

_____1) Fertile

_____2) Mother infertile

_____3) Father infertile

_____4) Infertility unclear, but failure to conceive

_____5) Information not available

_____6) Other (specify)

            _____
            _____
            _____

V.   Sex preference for adoptive child at time of application

_____1) Boy   _____3) No preference

_____2) Girl   _____4) Information not available

(If Preference Noted) Reasons for wanting a girl (boy):

_____
_____
_____
_____

VI.   Expressed motivation for adoption

_____1) Basic need of the child

_____2) Interest in human relations

_____3) Desire for more children or specific sex child

_____ 4) Special feeling for child

_____ 5) Other (specify)

                  _____

                  _____

                  _____

                  _____

VII.   Reservations at time when considering adopting (Specify)

                  _____

                  _____

                  _____

                  _____

                  _____

VIII.   Problematic areas in life situation of adoptive parents at time of adoptive study

	Mother	Father
1. Occupation adjustment	_____	_____
2. In-law relations	_____	_____
3. Finances	_____	_____
4. Sexual adjustment	_____	_____
5. Physical health	_____	_____
6. Relationship difficulties with "own" or previously adopted children	_____	_____
7. Other (specify)		
_____	_____	_____
_____	_____	_____
_____	_____	_____

IX.   Significant factors in developmental history of adoptive parents

	Mother	Father
1. Family broken during formative years	_____	_____
2. Physical disability and/or chronic ill health	_____	_____
3. Excessively strong attachment to either parent	_____	_____
4. Difficulty in school	_____	_____
5. Difficulty in peer relationships	_____	_____

134

			Mother	Father
6.	Difficulty in heterosexual adjustments		_____	_____
7.	Notable hostility to either parent		_____	_____
8.	Difficulty in sibling relationships		_____	_____
9.	Other (specify)			

_____ _____ _____
_____ _____ _____

X.   Adoptive worker's assessment for adoptive parenthood

_____ 1) Excellent   _____ 4) Doubtful

_____ 2) Good   _____ 5) Information not available

_____ 3) Fair

XI. Adoptive parents' reaction to presentation of child

Reaction	Mother	Father
Positive	_____	_____
Positive ambivalent	_____	_____
Neutral	_____	_____
Negative ambivalent	_____	_____
Negative	_____	_____
Information not available	_____	_____

Specific, significant reactions:

_____
_____
_____
_____

XII. Community's reaction to the adoption

1. Reactions of relatives to the adoption

_____
_____
_____
_____
_____

2. Reactions of friends and neighbors to the adoption

_____
_____
_____
_____
_____

3. (If the Parents Have Older Children) Reactions of other children to the adoption

_____
_____
_____
_____
_____

4. Reactions of other people in the community to the adoption

_____
_____
_____
_____
_____

XIII.   Child's adjustment to adoptive parents during first three months following placement

_____1) Adjusted readily without difficulty

_____2) Adjusted with some difficulty

_____3) Adjusted with considerable difficulty

_____4) Not yet adjusted

_____5) Information not available

XIV.   Adoptive parents' adjustment to role during first three months following placement

	Mother	Father
1. Adjusted readily without difficulty	_____	_____
2. Adjusted with some difficulty	_____	_____
3. Adjusted with considerable difficulty	_____	_____
4. Not yet adjusted	_____	_____

5. Information not available

_____ _____

(Significant aspects of adjustment)

_____
_____
_____
_____

XV. <u>Did the parents have reservations about finalizing the adoption?</u>

_____ Yes   _____ No   _____ Information unavailable

What reservations?

_____
_____
_____
_____

Appendix L

RESULTS OF STANDARD SCORE TESTS FOR DIFFERENCES OF PROPORTIONS FOR DATA SHOWN ON TABLE 4

RESULTS OF Z TEST FOR DATA SHOWN ON TABLE 4

Variable	Proportion of Adoptive Couples of Normal, White Infants	Proportion of TRA Couples	Z	P	Direction (when significant, or approaching significance)
Over 40	.198	.146	.70	.484	
Mixed marriage	.055	.049	.14	.889	
History of divorce	.077	.024	1.18	.238	
Health problems	.044	.049	.13	.897	
Two or more children in the home	.022	.610	7.74	.000	TRA more likely
Over 40	.956	.146	8.02	.000	IRA more likely
Mixed marriage	.165	.049	1.84	.066	IRA more likely
History of divorce	.132	.024	1.93	.054	IRA more likely
Health problems	.077	.049	.60	.549	
Two or more children in the home	.066	.610	6.80	.000	TRA more likely

(P values are for two-tailed test)

Reference: Social Statistics, by Hubert M. Blalock, New York: McGraw-Hill, pp. 176-178.

Appendix M

RESULTS OF WILCOXON MATCHED-PAIRS SIGNED-RANKS TEST FOR DATA
SHOWN ON TABLES 7, 8, 9, AND 16

	Variable	Z	P	Direction (when significant, or approaching significance)
Table 7:	Ages of IRA and TRA fathers at time of placement	.52	.603	
Table 8:	Ages of IRA and TRA mothers at time of placement	.27	.787	
Table 9:	Number of years married at time of placement	2.56	.010	TRA couples married longer
Table 16:	Ages of IRA and TRA children at time of placement	1.79	.073	TRA children older

(P values are for two-tailed test)

Reference: Nonparametric Statistics, by Sidney Siegel, New York: McGraw-Hill, 1956, pp. 75-83.

RESULTS OF WILCOXON MATCHED-PAIRS SIGNED-RANKS TEST FOR OUTCOME DATA
SHOWN ON TABLES 28, 30, 32, 34, AND 35

	Variable	Z	P	Direction (when significant, or approaching significance)
Table 28:	IRA and TRA couples' rating of level of satisfaction with overall adoptive experience	1.64	.101	
Table 30:	Interviewer's ratings of IRA and TRA couples' level of satisfaction with overall adoptive experience	1.02	3.08	
Table 32:	IRA and TRA couples' scores on Adoption Satisfaction Scale	.19	.849	
Table 34:	IRA and TRA couples' rating of ability to feel as loving toward adopted child as toward genetic child	2.02	.043	IRA couples assigned higher rating
Table 35:	IRA and TRA couples' rating of desire to repeat adoptive experience	1.02	.308	

(P values are for two-tailed test)

Reference: Nonparametric Statistics, by Sidney Siegel, New York: McGraw-Hill, 1956, pp. 75-83.

Appendix O

RESULTS OF KOLMOGOROV-SMIRNOV TEST FOR DATA SHOWN ON
TABLES 28 AND 29

Variable	Rejection Level	D	Direction
Rating of level of satisfaction with overall adoptive experience between TRA parents and adoptive parents of older children	For a two-tailed test (.05 level) a D score larger than .184 is needed to reject null hypothesis*	.215	TRA couples assigned higher rating

---

*Rejection score computed by formula:

$$1.36 \sqrt{\frac{N_1 + N_2}{N_1 N_2}}$$

where N = size of sample.

Reference: <u>Social Statistics</u>, by Hubert M. Blalock, New York: McGraw-Hill, pp. 203-206.

Appendix P

DISTRIBUTION OF STUDY GROUP BY PLACEMENT AGENCY IN WISCONSIN

Agency	No. of TRA Couples	No. of IRA Couples
Catholic Social Service in Madison	7	7
Catholic Social Service in Milwaukee	3	3
Children's Service Society of Wisconsin	5	4
Lutheran Social Services of Wisconsin and Upper Michigan	6	6
Milwaukee County Public Welfare Department	2	2
Regional Offices for the State Division of Family Services		
Green Bay Office	5	5
Madison Office	13	13
Milwaukee Office	2	1
Rhinelander Office	1	--
Totals	44	41

5 200